Ninja Foodi Grill Cookbook for Beginners

Easy & amazing Air Frying and Indoor Grilling Recipes

for Your Christmas, Holiday, and Daily Diet

Kimberly Hackler

© Copyright 2020 - All rights reserved.

The content contained within this book may not be reproduced, duplicated or transmitted without direct written permission from the author or the publisher.

Under no circumstances will any blame or legal responsibility be held against the publisher, or author, for any damages, reparation, or monetary loss due to the information contained within this book, either directly or indirectly.

Legal Notice:
This book is copyright protected. It is only for personal use. You cannot amend, distribute, sell, use, quote or paraphrase any part, or the content within this book, without the consent of the author or publisher.

Disclaimer Notice:
Please note the information contained within this document is for educational and entertainment purposes only. All effort has been executed to present accurate, up to date, reliable, complete information. No warranties of any kind are declared or implied. Readers acknowledge that the author is not engaged in the rendering of legal, financial, medical or professional advice. The content within this book has been derived from various sources. Please consult a licensed professional before attempting any techniques outlined in this book.

By reading this document, the reader agrees that under no circumstances is the author responsible for any losses, direct or indirect, that are incurred as a result of the use of the information contained within this document, including, but not limited to, errors, omissions, or inaccuracies.

Table of Contents

Introduction 5
   The Benefits of The Ninja Foodi Grill 5
   Using Your Ninja Foodi Grill 6
   Cleaning and Maintenance 8

Chapter 1: Breakfast Recipes 10
   Sausage and Kale Full Platter 10
   Breakfast Frittata 11
   Bacon Packed Stuffed Pepper 12
   Hearty Blistered Green Beans 13
   Elegant Pineapple Toast 14
   Juicy Potato Pancakes 15
   Bacon Stuffed Pepper 16
   Maple and Broccoli Platter 17
   Premium Broccoli and Garlic Meal 18
   Onion and Mushroom Meal 19
   Exciting Tomato Bacon Omelet 20

Chapter 2: Snacks and Appetizers Recipes 21
   Lobster Roll Bruschetta 21
   Swiss Ham Kabobs 22
   Grilled Basil Chicken and Tomatoes 23
   Dr Pepper Drumsticks 24
   Chiles Rellenos Grilled Chicken Tacos 25
   Grilled Spinach Feta Burgers 26
   Smoky Beer-Poached Grilled Corn 27

   Chili-Cheese Burgers 28
   Shishito and Shrimp Skewers with Chimichurri 29
   Mini Pineapple Pizzas 30
   Grilled Pistachio-Lemon Pesto Shrimp 31
   Sweet Sriracha Wings 32
   Grilled Beef-Mushroom Burgers 33
   Sun-Dried Tomato Turkey Burgers 34
   Grilled Sausage-Basil Pizzas 35

Chapter 3: Chicken and Poultry Recipes .. 36
   Turkey Tomato Burgers 36
   Spice Lover's Hot Pepper Wings 37
   Chicken Alfredo Apples Delight 38
   Mesmerizing Alfredo Apple Chicken 39
   Juicy BBQ Chicken 40
   Orange Grilled Chicken Meal 41
   Juicy Moroccan Chicken Roast 42
   Orange Flavored Chicken Delight 43
   Fancy Turkey Bacon Roast 44
   Juicy Moroccan Chicken Roast 45
   Turkey Burger with Tomato Dress 46

Chapter 4: Pork and Other Meat Recipes . 47
   Bourbon-y Pork Chops 47
   Lovely American Grilled Burger 48

Simple Coffee Flavored Steak 49
Delish Pineapple Steak 50
Authentic Korean Flank Steak 51
The Yogurt Lamb Skewers 52
Generous Pesto Beef Meal 53
Cool Avocado Steak Salad 54
Italian Basil Pizza 55
Juicy Korean Chii Pork Delight 56

Chapter 5: Fish and Seafood Recipes 57

Salmon and Dill Sauce Meal 57
Freshly Baked Haddock 58
Italian Garlic Salmon 59
Daring Spicy Grilled Shrimp 60
Paprika Grilled Shrimp 61
Subtly Roasted BBQ Shrimp 62
Coho Glazed Salmon 63
Spicy Buttered Salmon 64
Spicy Cajun Shrimp 65
Crispy Crab Patty 66
Mustard-y Crisped Up Cod 67
Easy BBQ Roast Shrimp 68
Swordfish with Caper Sauce 69

Chapter 6: Vegetarian and Vegan Recipes. 70

Healthy Fruit Salad 70
Stuffed Up Cheesy Zucchini 71
Grilled Veggies with Mustard Vinaigrette.. 72
Exciting Olive and Spinach 73
Bruschetta from the Grill 74
Shishito Pepper Charred 75
Blissful Simple Beans 76
Toasty Broccoli 77
Honey-Licious Asparagus 78
Honey and Herb Charred Carrots 79
Broccoli and Torn Arugula 80
Grilled Tomato Salsa 81
Italian Rosemary Potatoes 82
Spicy Grilled Eggplant 83
Rice & Vegetable Stuffed Peppers 84

Chapter 7: Desserts Recipes 85

Juicy Grilled Pound Cakes 85
Granola Flavored Healthy Muffin 86
Marshmallow Banana Boat 87
Blueberry Cobbler Delight 88
Excellent Rum Sundae 89
The Original Corn Biscuit 90
Air Crisped Delicious Mac and Cheese 91
Rummy Pineapple Sunday 92
Fiery Cajun Eggplant Dish 93
Flattering Banana Chips 94
Premium Tomato and Bacon Omelet 95

Introduction

Becoming "Smart" has changed the entire narrative and overall lifestyle of man in the modern-day world. From gadgets to appliances, to "Smart" automated homes, the 21st-century lifestyle has got stern domination of the internet. Considering the reach of the technological advancements, our kitchen has also been impacted very much overtime with the introduction of Smart devices & appliances for cooking. The Ninja Foodi Grill is one such Smart device that has changed the horizons of the cooking world. This is because it can perform grilling, baking, roasting, dehydrating, and air crisping, etc. The amalgamation of so many cooking techniques in one single device is a significant breakthrough in the cooking world. This is why the Ninja Foodi Grill is going to knock out all other conventional cooking appliances from your kitchen. Furthermore, it is certified as "smoke-free," giving you an ultra-convenient and healthy cooking solution.

The Benefits of The Ninja Foodi Grill

Whether it is a trend or the general convenience of it, more people are appreciating smaller and more portable indoor cookers due to a number of benefits from owning one.

Easy to clean and operate – Indoor grills are plug and play appliances making them user-friendly to a wider demographic. The cooking components are coated with a non-stick ceramic material that can be effortlessly taken apart and cleaned using a standard dishwasher.

Smokeless – This is probably one of the best things about indoor electric grills. People who do not have any access to open areas can still enjoy grilling since it does not produce smoke like standard grillers.

Multi-function – Most indoor cookers come with various functionalities giving you more value for your money. It can also eliminate the need to purchase other appliances and save you essential kitchen space.

Compact – Electric grills are small enough to fit most kitchen counters and tables. It is also portable enough to be easily transported or moved around.

Capable of high temperatures – A wide range of temperature settings let you cook a variety of foods from char-grilled vegetables to restaurant-level steaks. Unlike other tabletop cookers, the Ninja Grill will let you cook frozen foods without the need to defrost. It can also get as hot as 500 to 510 degrees Fahrenheit.

Browns and crisps food – Indoor grills like the Ninja Foodi use the circulating hot air to cook the food thoroughly. This creates delectable flavors through a browning process called the

Maillard reaction. Similar to convection ovens and toasters, the Ninja Foodi is excellent at making food crunchy when you need it to be.

Grill marks - Like traditional outdoor grills, indoor grills can also give meat and other foods those appetizing grill marks. Although, the Ninja Foodi's grill marks are curved, unlike the typical straight markings you get from regular outdoor grills.

Using Your Ninja Foodi Grill

When you are cooking for the first time with your Foodi grill, you must first wash the detachable cooking parts with warm soapy water to remove any oil and debris. Let it air dry and put them back inside once you are ready to cook. An easy-to-follow instruction guide comes with each unit, so make sure to go over it prior to cooking.

Position your grill on a level and secure surface. Leave at least 6 inches of space around it, especially at the back where the air intake vent and air socket are located. Ensure that the splatter guard is installed whenever the grill is in use. This is a wire mesh that covers the heating element on the inside of the lid.

For Grilling

Plug your unit into an outlet and power on the grill.

Use the grill grate over the cooking pot and choose the grill function. This has four default temperature settings of low at 400 degrees F, medium at 450 degrees F, high at 500 degrees F, and max at 510 degrees F.

Set the time needed to cook. You may check the grilling cheat sheet that comes with your unit to guide you with the time and temperature settings. It is best to check the food regularly depending on the doneness you prefer and to avoid overcooking.

Once the required settings are selected, press start and wait for the digital display to show 'add food'. The unit will start to preheat similar to an oven and will show the progress through the display. This step takes about 8 minutes.

If you need to check the food or flip it, the timer will pause and resume once the lid is closed.

The screen will show 'Done' once the timer and cooking has completed. Turn off the unit and unplug the device. Leave the hood open to let the unit cool faster.

For Air Crisping

Put the crisper basket in and close the lid.

Press the air crisp or air fry option then the start button. The default temperature is set at 390° F and will preheat at about 3 minutes. You can adjust the temperature and time by pressing the buttons beside these options.

If you do not need to preheat, just press the air crisp button a second time and the display will show you the 'add food' message.

Put the food inside and shake or turn every 10 minutes. Use oven mitts or tongs with silicone tips when doing this.

For Baking

Remove the grates and use the cooking pot.

Choose the bake setting and set your preferred temperature and time. Preheating will take about 3 minutes.

Once done with preheating, you may put the ingredients directly on the cooking pot, or you may use your regular baking tray. An 8-inch baking tray can fit inside as well as similar-sized oven-safe containers.

For Roasting

Remove the grill grates and use the cooking pot that comes with the unit. You may also purchase their roasting rack for this purpose.

Press the roast option and set the timer between 1 to 4 hours depending on the recipe requirements. The Foodi will preheat for 3 minutes regardless of the time you have set.

Once ready, place the meat directly on the roasting pot or rack.

Check occasionally for doneness. A meat thermometer is another useful tool to get your meats perfectly cooked.

For Dehydrating

Place the first layer of food directly on the cooking pot.

Add the crisper basket and add one more layer.

Choose the dehydrate setting and set the timer between 7 to 10 hours.

You may check the progress from time to time.

For cooking frozen foods:

Choose the medium heat, which is 450° F using the grill option. You may also use the air crisp option if you are cooking fries, vegetables, and other frozen foods.

Set the time needed for your recipe. Add a few minutes to compensate for the thawing.

Flip or shake after a few minutes to cook the food evenly.

Cleaning and Maintenance

Components are dishwasher-safe and are fabricated with a non-stick ceramic coating, to make clean-up and maintenance easier. Plus, the grill conveniently comes with a plastic cleaning brush with a scraper at the other end.

Cleaning Tips

It might appear very tricky to thoroughly clean the Ninja Foodi Grill, but it is not complicated at all. You merely need to follow certain easy steps, and your device is ready to go for another round. It is recommended to thoroughly clean the Ninja Foodi Grill after every use. To clean the unit thoroughly and safely, follow the following guidelines:

- Let the device cool down before cleaning.
- Unplug the device from the power source.
- For quick cooling, keep the hood of the device open.
- The grill gate, splatter shield, crisper basket, cooking pot, cleaning brush, and the rest of the accessories are certified as **DISHWASHER SAFE**.
- The thermometer is not dishwasher safe.
- Rinse the accessories like splatter shield, grill gate, etc. for better cleaning results.
- Use the cleaning brush included with the device for handwashing.
- For cleaning baked-on cheese or sauces, utilize the other end of the cleaning brush for being used as a scrapper for effective hand washing.
- Either towel-dry or air-dry all the components after hand washing.
- **DO NOT** dip the main unit in any liquid, including water.
- **DO NOT** use any rasping cleaners or tools.
- **NEVER** use any sort of liquid cleaning solution near or on the thermometer.
- Always use a cotton swab or compressed air to avoid any damage to the jack.

In case of any grease or food residue left and stuck on the components of the Ninja Foodi Grill, follow the following cleaning steps thoroughly:

1. If the residue is stuck on the splatter shield, grill gate, or any other accessory or part, soak it in warm soapy water solution before cleaning.

2. The splatter should be cleaned thoroughly after every use. For better cleansing, soak it in warm water overnight will assists efficiently in softening the stuck grease or sauces.

3. You can also deep clean the splatter shield by thoroughly immersing it in water and further boiling it for approximately 10 minutes.

4. Moreover, you can then rinse it effectively with room temperature water and let it dry properly for better results.

For deep cleaning the thermometer, you can soak both the silicone grip and the stainless-steel tip in a container full of warm water. But, keep in mind that the jack or the cord **SHOULD NOT** be immersed or soaked in any solution, including water, as mentioned earlier. The thermometer holder of the Ninja Foodi Grill is clearly **HANDWASH** only.

Maintenance Tips

Always keep your unit clean, especially before putting in a new batch for cooking. You should clean the parts and the unit after each use.

Never use cleaning instruments or chemicals that are too harsh and can damage the coating.

Keep the electrical cords away from children and any traffic in your kitchen.

Avoid getting the unit and electrical components wet and place it away from areas that constantly get soaked or damp.

At all times, unplug the unit when not in use.

Chapter 1: Breakfast Recipes

Sausage and Kale Full Platter

(Prepping time: 10 minutes| Cooking time: 10 minutes |For 4 servings)

Ingredients

- 1 medium sweet yellow onion
- 4 medium eggs
- 4 sausage links
- 2 cups kale, chopped
- 1 cup mushrooms
- Olive oil as needed

Directions

1. Set Ninja Foodi Grill to "HIGH" and set the timer to 5 minutes
2. Once you hear a beep, arrange sausages over the grill grate
3. Cook for 2 minutes, flip and cook for 3 minutes more
4. Take the sausages out, take a baking pan, and spread onion, kale, mushrooms, sausages
5. Crack eggs on top
6. Arrange pan inside your grill, set BAKE mode with temperature to 350 degrees F
7. Bake for 5 minutes, serve and enjoy!

Nutrition Facts Per Serving

Calories: 236, Fat: 12 g, Saturated Fat: 2 g, Carbohydrates: 17 g, Fiber: 4 g, Sodium: 369 mg, Protein: 18 g

Breakfast Frittata

(Prepping time: 10 minutes| Cooking time:10 minutes |For 4 servings)

Ingredients

- 4 cremini mushrooms, sliced
- ½ cup cheddar cheese, shredded
- ½ bell pepper, seeded and diced
- 4 large eggs
- ¼ cup whole milk
- ½ onion, chopped
- Salt and pepper to taste

Directions

1. Whisk in eggs, milk into a medium-sized bowl
2. Season with salt and pepper
3. Add bell pepper, onion, mushroom, cheese and mix them well
4. Pre-heat your Ninja Foodi by pressing the "BAKE" option and setting it to 400 Degrees F
5. Set the timer to 10 minutes
6. Allow it to pre-heat until it beeps
7. Pour Egg Mixture into your Ninja Foodi Bake Pan and spread well
8. Transfer to Grill and close the lid
9. Bake for 10 minutes
10. Serve and enjoy!

Nutrition Facts Per Serving

Calories: 153, Fat: 10 g, Saturated Fat: 5 g, Carbohydrates: 5 g, Fiber: 1 g, Sodium: 177 mg, Protein: 11 g

Bacon Packed Stuffed Pepper

(Prepping time: 5 - 10 minutes| Cooking time: 15 minutes |For 4 servings)

Ingredients

- Parsley, chopped for garnish
- Salt and pepper to taste
- 4 bell pepper, seeded and tops removed
- 1 cup cheddar cheese, shredded
- 4 large eggs
- 4 slices bacon, cooked and chopped

Directions

1. Take the bell peppers, divide cheese and bacon between them
2. Crack an egg into each of the bell peppers, season them with salt and pepper
3. Pre-heat your Ninja Foodi to 390 degrees F in AIR CRISP mode
4. Set your timer to 15 minutes, wait until you hear a beep
5. Transfer bell pepper to your Grill and lock lid; cook for 15 minutes until the egg whites are set and yolks are slightly runny
6. Remove pepper from the basket and garnish with parsley
7. Enjoy!

Nutrition Facts Per Serving

Calories: 326, Fat: 23 g, Saturated Fat: 10 g, Carbohydrates: 10 g, Fiber: 2 g, Sodium: 781 mg, Protein: 22 g

Hearty Blistered Green Beans

(Prepping time: 5 - 10 minutes| Cooking time: 10 minutes |For 4 servings)

Ingredients

- Salt and pepper to taste
- Pinch of red pepper flakes
- 1 lemon, juiced
- 2 tablespoons oil
- 1 pound green beans, trimmed

Directions

1. Take a medium-sized bowl, add green beans
2. Pre-heat your Ninja Foodi Grill to MAX, setting a timer for 10 minutes
3. Once you hear the beep, add green beans to the Grate
4. Lock lid and grill for 8-10 minutes, making sure to toss from time to time to ensure that they are blistered well
5. Squeeze a bit of lemon on top and sprinkle red pepper flakes, season with salt and pepper
6. Enjoy!

Nutrition Facts Per Serving

Calories: 100, Fat: 7 g, Saturated Fat: 1 g, Carbohydrates: 10 g, Fiber: 4 g, Sodium: 30 mg, Protein: 2 g

Elegant Pineapple Toast

(Prepping time: 5-10 minutes| Cooking time:15 minutes |For 4 servings)

Ingredients

- Cooking spray as needed
- ½ cup cooking flakes
- 10 slices pineapple
- 1 cup of coconut milk
- 3 large whole egg
- ¼ cup milk
- ¼ cup of sugar
- 10 bread slices

Directions

1. Take a medium-sized bowl and whisk in eggs, coconut milk, sugar and stir well
2. Dip your pineapple slices into the mixture and let them sit for 2 minutes
3. Pre-heat your Ninja Foodi Grill in MED settings, giving timer to 15 minutes
4. Transfer prepared slices to Grill and cook for 2 minutes, flip and cook for 2 minutes more
5. Repeat with all the slices

Nutrition Facts Per Serving

Calories: 202, Fat: 15 g, Saturated Fat: 3 g, Carbohydrates: 49 g, Fiber: 3 g, Sodium: 524 mg, Protein: 8 g

Juicy Potato Pancakes

(Prepping time: 5 - 10 minutes| Cooking time: 24 minutes |For 4 servings)

Ingredients

- 4 medium potatoes, peeled and cleaned
- 1 medium onion, chopped
- 1 egg, beaten
- ¼ cup milk
- 2 tablespoons unsalted butter
- ½ teaspoon garlic powder
- ¼ teaspoon salt
- 3 tablespoons flour
- Salt and pepper to taste

Directions

1. Take your potatoes and peel them well
2. Shred the potatoes and soak the shredded potatoes under water, drain them
3. Take another bowl and add milk, butter, eggs, garlic powder, pepper, salt and add flour, mix well
4. Add shredded potatoes
5. Pre-heat your Ninja Foodi to 390 degrees F in AIR CRISP mode, set the timer to 24 minutes
6. Once you hear a beep, add ¼ cup of potato pancake batter
7. Cook for 12 minutes, until you have a good texture
8. Cook with remaining batter
9. Enjoy!

Nutrition Facts Per Serving

Calories: 240, Fat: 11 g, Saturated Fat: 3 g, Carbohydrates: 33 g, Fiber: 4 g, Sodium: 259 mg, Protein: 6 g

Bacon Stuffed Pepper

(Prepping time: 10 minutes| Cooking time:15 minutes |For 4 servings)

Ingredients

- 4 slices bacon, cooked and chopped
- 4 large eggs
- 1 cup cheddar cheese, shredded
- 4 bell peppers, seeded and tops removed
- Salt and pepper to taste
- Chopped parsley, for garnish

Directions

1. Take your bell peppers and divide cheese and bacon between them
2. Crack an egg into each of the bell peppers
3. Season them with salt and pepper
4. Pre-heat your Ninja Foodi by pressing the "AIR CRISP" option and setting it to 390 Degrees F
5. Set your timer to 15 minutes
6. Allow it to pre-heat until it beeps
7. Transfer bell pepper to your cooking basket and transfer to Foodi Grill
8. Lock the lid and cook for 10-15 minutes until egg whites are cooked well until the yolks are slightly runny
9. Remove peppers from the basket and garnish with parsley
10. Serve and enjoy!

Nutrition Facts Per Serving

Calories: 326, Fat: 23 g, Saturated Fat: 10 g, Carbohydrates: 10 g, Fiber: 2 g, Sodium: 781 mg, Protein: 22 g

Maple and Broccoli Platter

(Prepping time: 5-10 minutes| Cooking time:10 minutes |For 4 servings)

Ingredients

- Red pepper flakes and sesame seeds for garnish
- 2 teaspoons maple syrup
- 4 tablespoon balsamic vinegar
- 2 tablespoons canola oil
- 4 tablespoons soy sauce
- 2 heads broccoli, cut into florets

Directions

1. Take a shallow mixing bowl and add vinegar, soy sauce, oil, maple syrup and whisk the whole mixture thoroughly
2. Add broccoli to the mix and let it sit for a while
3. Set your Ninja Foodi Grill to "MAX" mode and set the timer to 10 minutes
4. Once you hear the beep, add prepared broccoli over Grill Grate
5. Let it cook until the timer reaches 0
6. Top with sesame seeds, pepper flakes if you prefer some heat
7. Enjoy!

Nutrition Facts Per Serving

Calories: 141, Fat: 7 g, Saturated Fat: 1 g, Carbohydrates: 14 g, Fiber: 4 g, Sodium: 853 mg, Protein: 4 g

Premium Broccoli and Garlic Meal

(Prepping time: 5-10 minutes| Cooking time: 10 minutes |For 4 servings)

Ingredients

- 2 heads broccoli, cut into florets
- 4 tablespoon soy sauce
- 2 tablespoon canola oil
- 4 tablespoon balsamic vinegar
- 2 teaspoon maple syrup
- Red pepper flakes and sesame seeds for garnish

Directions

1. First, take a mixing bowl and put vinegar, soy sauce, oil, maple syrup, and whisk, then mix all those ingredients.

2. Onward add broccoli to the mixture and keep them aside for a while.

3. Take your Ninja Foodi Grill and set this in the "MAX" mode with 10 minutes timer.

4. After hearing the first beep add the broccoli which was prepared before, over the Grill Grate.

5. Keep all those in the cooking process until the timer is 0.

6. Garnish with sesame seeds, pepper flakes if you like to taste spicy.

7. Enjoy.

Nutrition Facts Per Serving

Calories: 141, Fat: 7g, Carbohydrate: 14g, Protein: 4g, Sodium: 853 mg, Fiber: 4g, Saturated Fat: 1g

Onion and Mushroom Meal

(Prepping time: 5 - 10 minutes| Cooking time: 10 minutes |For 4 servings)

Ingredients

- ½ cup cheese, shredded
- 4 cremini mushrooms, sliced
- ½ onion, chopped
- ½ bell pepper, seeded and diced
- Salt and pepper to taste
- ¼ cup whole milk
- 4 large eggs

Directions

1. Take a medium-sized bowl, whisk in the egg, milk, salt, and pepper
2. Add bell pepper, onion, mushroom, cheese and mix well
3. Preheat your Grill to 400 degrees F in Bake mode, with the timer set to 400 degrees F
4. Once you hear the beep, pour egg mixture in Ninja Foodi Pan and grill until the timer runs out
5. Serve and enjoy once you see a golden texture

Nutrition Facts Per Serving

Calories: 153, Fat: 10 g, Saturated Fat: 5 g, Carbohydrates: 5 g, Fiber: 1 g, Sodium: 177 mg, Protein: 11 g

Exciting Tomato Bacon Omelet

(Prepping time: 5-10 minutes| Cooking time:10 minutes |For 4 servings)

Ingredients

- Salt and pepper to taste
- 1 tablespoon olive oil
- 1 tablespoon parsley, chopped
- 4 tomatoes, cubed
- ¼ pound bacon, cooked and chopped
- 4 whole eggs, whisked

Directions

1. Take a small-sized pan and place it over medium level heat, add bacon and Sauté for about 2 minutes until finely crisped

2. Take another bowl and add the Sautéed bowl and add rest of the listed ingredients, sprinkle cheese and stir

3. Pre-heat your Ninja Foodi Grill using BAKE option to a temperature of 400 degrees F for about 10 minutes

4. Wait until you hear a beep

5. Transfer the prepared mixture into your baking dish and transfer to your Grill, bake for 8 minutes

6. Serve once done, enjoy!

Nutrition Facts Per Serving

Calories: 311, Fat: 16g, Saturated Fat: 4 g, Carbohydrates: 23 g, Fiber: 2 g, Sodium: 149 mg, Protein: 22 g

Chapter 2: Snacks and Appetizers Recipes

Lobster Roll Bruschetta

(Prepping time: 10 minutes| Cooking time:15 minutes |For 20 servings)

Ingredients

- 2 (8-oz.) lobster tails
- Cooking spray
- 1/2 cup red wine vinegar
- 1 tablespoon of granulated sugar
- 1/8 teaspoon of crushed red pepper
- 2 small shallots, peeled and cut into thin rings
- 1 (10-oz.) French bread baguette split lengthwise
- 1/4 cup extra-virgin olive oil
- 2 cups chopped tomatoes (2 large tomatoes)
- 1 1/2 tablespoons fresh lemon juice
- 1 tablespoon chopped fresh flat-leaf parsley
- 1/2 teaspoon kosher salt
- 1 tablespoon chopped fresh basil
- 1/2 teaspoon freshly ground black pepper
- 6 tablespoons canola mayonnaise

Directions

1. Mix together vinegar, sugar, and crushed red pepper in a medium-sized bowl safe for microwave use. Microwave the mixture at HIGH until hot and sugar has melted for about 1-2 minutes. Add shallots. Let stand 5 minutes; drain.

2. Preheat the grill for 8 minutes before use.

3. Use a sharp knife and cut lobster tails in half lengthwise. Coat the flesh with cooking spray. Place the lobster tails while flesh side down on the grill. Grill while uncovered until the grill marks appear, about 4 minutes. Turn the lobster tails over, and grill, while uncovered until flesh, is opaque for about 2 minutes. Remove it from the grill and cool for 10 minutes.

4. Meanwhile, lightly coat the bread with cooking oil. Cut each bread piece in half. Place bread while cut side down on the grill; grill while uncovered until toasted for about 1 to 2 minutes.

5. Remove meat from lobster tails, and chop. Discard the shells. Stir together the lobster meat, lemon juice, oil, tomato, parsley, basil, salt, and black pepper in a medium bowl.

6. Spread 1 and 1/2 tablespoons mayonnaise on cut side of each bread piece; top evenly with lobster mixture and pickled shallots. Cut each bread piece into five slices.

Nutrition Facts Per Serving

Calories 106, Total Fat 6g, Total Carbs 9g, Total Protein 4g

Swiss Ham Kabobs

(Prepping time: 10 minutes| Cooking time:10-15 minutes |For 4 servings)

Ingredients

- 1/2 cup orange marmalade
- 1 tablespoon prepared mustard
- 1 can (20 ounces) Dole pineapple chunks
- 1/4 teaspoon ground cloves
- 1/2 pound Swiss cheese, cut into 1-inch cubes
- 1 pound fully cooked ham, cut into 1-inch cubes
- 1 medium green pepper, cut into 1-inch pieces, optional

Directions

1. Drain pineapple while reserving two tablespoons juice and set pineapple aside. Take a small bowl and mix marmalade, cloves, mustard, and reserved pineapple juice in it. On eight metal or soaked wooden skewers, alternately thread ham, cheese, pineapple, and, if desired, green pepper.

2. Preheat the Ninja Foodi grill for 8 minutes before using it. Place kabobs on the greased grill. Grill while uncovered over medium heat or broil 4 in. From heat 5-7 minutes or until heated through, turning and frequently basting with marmalade sauce. Serve with remaining sauce.

Nutrition Facts Per Serving

Calories 523, Total Fat 19g, Total Carbs 55g, Total Protein 33g

Grilled Basil Chicken and Tomatoes

(Prepping time: 15 minutes| Cooking time:10 minutes |For 4 servings)

Ingredients

- 1 garlic clove, minced
- 1/2 teaspoon salt
- 3/4 cup balsamic vinegar
- 1/4 cup tightly packed fresh basil leaves
- 2 tablespoons olive oil
- 8 plum tomatoes
- 4 boneless skinless chicken breast halves (4 ounces each)

Directions

1. For making the marinade, put the first five ingredients in a blender. Cut four tomatoes and add to blender; cover and process until thoroughly blended. Halve the remaining tomatoes for grilling purposes.

2. In a bowl, mix chicken and 2/3 cup of marinade; refrigerate it while being covered for1 hour, turning occasionally — keep the remaining marinade for serving.

3. Preheat the grill for 8 minutes before putting anything in it. Place chicken on the oiled grill over medium heat; discard marinade remaining in bowl. Grill chicken while covering it until the temperature reads 165°F for 4-6 minutes per side. Grill the tomatoes while covered over medium heat until lightly browned for 2-4 minutes per side. Serve chicken and tomatoes with reserved marinade.

Nutrition Facts Per Serving

Calories 173, Total Fat 5g, Total Carbs 8g, Total Protein 24g

Dr Pepper Drumsticks

(Prepping time: 20 minutes| Cooking time:30 minutes |For 6 servings)

Ingredients

- 2 tablespoons brown sugar
- 2 tablespoons bourbon
- 1 cup ketchup
- 2/3 cup Dr Pepper
- 4 teaspoons barbecue seasoning
- 1/8 teaspoon salt
- 1/4 teaspoon celery salt, optional
- 1 tablespoon Worcestershire sauce
- 2 teaspoons dried minced onion
- 12 chicken drumsticks

Directions

1. Take a saucepan and mix the first 8 ingredients; stir in celery salt if desired. Bring to a boil. Reduce heat to sim while uncovered for 8-10 minutes or until slightly thickened, stirring frequently.

2. Preheat the grill for 8 minutes before use. Cook chicken while covered over medium-low heat for 15 minutes on the oiled grill. Turn; grill 15-20 minutes longer or until the temperature reads 170°F-175°F, occasionally brushing with sauce mixture.

Nutrition Facts Per Serving

Calories 300, Total Fat 12g, Total Carbs 19g, Total Protein 29g

Chiles Rellenos Grilled Chicken Tacos

(Prepping time: 40 minutes| Cooking time:30 minutes |For 8 servings)

Ingredients

- 1/3 cup olive oil
- 2 teaspoons salt
- 1/3 cup lime juice
- 1/3 cup red wine vinegar
- 2 teaspoons sugar
- 2 teaspoons pepper
- 2 pounds boneless skinless chicken thighs
- 1 cup coarsely chopped fresh cilantro
- 2 tablespoons finely chopped chipotle peppers in adobo sauce

Tacos:

- 4 poblano peppers
- 8 flour tortillas (8 inches)
- 1 tablespoon olive oil
- 2 cups shredded Monterey Jack cheese

Directions

1. Take a small bowl and whisk the first six ingredients until blended; stir in cilantro and chipotles. Transfer 2/3 cup marinade to a large resealable plastic bag. Add the chicken and seal the bag. Turn to coat. Refrigerate 8 hours or overnight. Cover and refrigerate remaining marinade for tossing with grilled chicken.

2. Brush poblanos with 1 tablespoon oil. Preheat the grill for 8 minutes before use. Grill peppers, covered, over high heat 8-10 minutes or until they are blistered and black, turning as required. Immediately place the peppers in a small bowl; let it stand while covered for 20 minutes. Reduce grill temperature to medium heat.

3. Drain chicken, discarding marinade in bag. Grill chicken, covered, over medium heat 6-8 minutes on each side or until the temperature reads 170°F.

4. Peel off and discard charred skin from peppers. Cut peppers lengthwise in half; carefully remove stems and seeds. Cut chicken into slices. Warm reserved marinade; add chicken and toss to coat.

5. To assemble, place one pepper half in center of each tortilla; top with 1/2 cup chicken and 1/4 cup cheese. Fold tortillas in half overfilling. Grill while covered on medium heat for 2-3 minutes on each side or until heated through.

Nutrition Facts Per Serving

Calories 525, Total Fat 29g, Total Carbs 33g, Total Protein 33g

Grilled Spinach Feta Burgers

(Prepping time: 25 minutes| Cooking time:15-20 minutes |For 8 servings)

Ingredients

- 1 tablespoon olive oil
- 2-1/2 cups fresh baby spinach, coarsely chopped
- 3 garlic cloves, minced
- 2 shallots, chopped
- 2/3 cup crumbled feta cheese
- 1/2 teaspoon salt
- 1/4 teaspoon pepper
- 2 pounds lean ground beef (90% lean)
- 3/4 teaspoon Greek seasoning
- 8 whole-wheat hamburger buns, split
- Optional toppings: refrigerated tzatziki sauce, fresh baby spinach, and tomato slices

Directions

1. Preheat the grill for 8 minutes before cooking anything in it. In a large skillet, heat oil over medium-high heat. Add shallots; cook and stir until tender, 1-2 minutes. Add spinach and garlic; cook until spinach is wilted, 30-45 seconds longer. Transfer to a large bowl; cool slightly.

2. Stir feta cheese and seasonings into the spinach. Add beef; mix lightly but thoroughly. Shape into eight 1/2-in.-thick patties.

3. Grill burgers while covered over medium heat until the temperature reads 160°F, 6-8 minutes on each side. Grill buns over medium heat, cut side down, until toasted, 30-60 seconds. Serve burgers on buns. If desired, add toppings.

Nutrition Facts Per Serving

Calories 347, Total Fat 15g, Total Carbs 25g, Total Protein 28g

Smoky Beer-Poached Grilled Corn

(Prepping time: 10 minutes| Cooking time:20 minutes |For 8 servings)

Ingredients

- 8 ears of fresh sweet corn, husks pulled back
- 3 tablespoons unsalted butter, softened
- 1 (1/2-inch-thick) sweet onion slices
- Cooking spray
- 5 (12-oz.) bottles of lager beer
- 2 teaspoons grainy mustard
- 1 1/8 teaspoons kosher salt
- 1/4 teaspoon black pepper
- 1/2 cup malt vinegar

Directions

1. Preheat the Ninja Foodi grill for 8 minutes before use. Coat the onion slices with cooking spray. Grill while uncovered and until charred and tender for 3 to 4 minutes per side. Transfer the onion rings to a small bowl and cover it with plastic wrap. Let stand until fully tender for about 10 minutes. Keep the grill hot.

2. Boil the beer in a large Dutch oven over medium-high. Add corn and return to a boil. Remove from the heat. Cover and let it stand until corn is mostly tender 5 to 8 minutes. Drain.

3. Finely chop onion slices. Stir together the onions, butter, mustard, salt, and pepper. Shape into a 4-inch log; wrap in plastic wrap, and chill until ready to use.

4. Grill corn while uncovered with often turning, until charred and fully tender for 5-6 minutes. Drizzle hot corn with vinegar, and serve with butter mixture.

Nutrition Facts Per Serving

Calories 150, Total Fat 6g, Total Carbs 20g, Total Protein 4g

Chili-Cheese Burgers

(Prepping time: 10 minutes| Cooking time:15 minutes |For 4 servings)

Ingredients

- 1 tablespoon chili powder
- 1 pound ground beef
- 1/2 cup shredded cheddar cheese
- 6 tablespoons chili sauce, divided
- 4 hamburger buns, split
- Lettuce leaves, tomato slices and mayonnaise, optional

Directions

1. Take a large bowl and combine cheese, two tablespoons chili sauce and chili powder in it. Add beef and mix lightly and thoroughly. Shape into four 1/2-in.-thick patties.

2. Preheat the grill for 8 minutes before use. Grill burgers while covered over medium heat or broil 4 in. From heat 4 to 5 minutes on both sides or until the temperature reads 160°F. Serve on buns with remaining chili sauce and lettuce, tomato, and mayonnaise if desired.

Nutrition Facts Per Serving

Calories 395, Total Fat 19g, Total Carbs 29g, Total Protein 27g

Shishito and Shrimp Skewers with Chimichurri

(Prepping time: 15 minutes| Cooking time:10 minutes |For 4 servings)

Ingredients

- 2 garlic cloves
- 1/2 teaspoon grated lemon rind
- 1 cup firmly packed fresh flat-leaf parsley leaves
- 1 cup firmly packed fresh cilantro leaves
- 1/4 cup firmly packed fresh basil leaves
- 3/4 teaspoon kosher salt, divided
- 2 tablespoons fresh lemon juice
- 1/4 teaspoon crushed red pepper
- 4 tablespoons extra-virgin olive oil, divided
- 1 1/2 pounds large shrimp (about 24), peeled and deveined (tails on)
- 16 (2-in.) shishito peppers (about 3 oz.)
- 1/4 teaspoon black pepper
- Cooking spray

Directions

1. Preheat the grill for 8 minutes before use.

2. Process parsley, garlic, cilantro, basil, in a food processor until they are finely chopped. Add lemon rind, juice, crushed red pepper, three tablespoons oil, and 1/4 teaspoon salt; process until finely chopped and well combined.

3. Toss together shrimp and 1/4 cup of herb mixture. Thread 4 shrimps onto each of 6 (8-inch) skewers and thread 8 peppers onto each of 2 (8-inch) skewers. Sprinkle skewers with remaining 1 tablespoon oil; sprinkle with black pepper and remaining 1/2 teaspoon salt.

4. Place skewers on the grill coated with cooking spray. Grill until shrimp is done and peppers are charred for 2 to 3 minutes per side. Brush skewers with remaining herb mixture before serving.

Nutrition Facts Per Serving

Calories 260, Total Fat 16g, Total Carbs 5g, Total Protein 24g

Mini Pineapple Pizzas

(Prepping time: 10 minutes| Cooking time: 20 minutes |For 8 servings)

Ingredients

- 2/3 cup part-skim mozzarella cheese, shredded
- 1/2 cup lower-sodium pizza sauce (such as Rao's)
- 2 tablespoons thinly sliced black olives
- 1 medium pineapple, peeled and cored
- 2 tablespoons canola oil, divided
- 8 (1-oz.) slices Canadian bacon
- 1/2 cup thinly sliced red onion
- 3 tablespoons chopped fresh basil
- 1/2 teaspoon crushed red pepper flakes (optional)

Directions

1. Preheat the grill for 8 minutes before use.

2. Heat a grill pan over medium-high. Slice pineapple into 8 (1/2-inch) rounds. Using 1 ½ tablespoon of oil, brush oil on both sides of pineapple rounds. Working in batches, place pineapple rounds on the grill pan, and cook 3 minutes on each side, until char marks appear. Transfer to a rimmed baking sheet.

3. Place Canadian bacon slices on grill pan and cook, 1 to 2 minutes on each side, until heated through. Set aside.

4. Heat remaining 1 ½ teaspoons oil in a separate nonstick skillet over medium. Add onion and cook, 3 to 4 minutes, often stirring, until softened.

5. Top each pineapple round with 1 tsp of Cheese. Place one slice Canadian bacon on top of the cheese. Top each with one tablespoon pizza sauce and one tablespoon cheese. Top evenly with onion and black olives. Grill on high for 2-3 minutes, until cheese is bubbly and melted. Sprinkle basil and crushed red pepper flakes evenly overtop.

Nutrition Facts Per Serving

Calories 143, Total Fat 7g, Total Carbs 12g, Total Protein 8g

Grilled Pistachio-Lemon Pesto Shrimp

(Prepping time: 45 minutes| Cooking time:5-10 minutes |For 8 servings)

Ingredients

- 1/3 cup shelled pistachios
- 2 tablespoons lemon juice
- 3/4 cup fresh arugula
- 1/2 cup minced fresh parsley
- 1 garlic clove, peeled
- 1/2 cup olive oil
- 1/4 cup shredded Parmesan cheese
- 1/4 teaspoon grated lemon zest
- 1/4 teaspoon salt
- 1/8 teaspoon pepper
- 1-1/2 pounds uncooked jumbo shrimp, peeled and deveined

Directions

1. Put the first six elements in a food processor and pulse until they are finely chopped. Continue processing while gradually adding oil in a steady stream. Add Parmesan cheese, salt, and pepper; pulse just until combined. Transfer 1/3 cup pesto to a large bowl. Add shrimp and toss to coat. Refrigerate while covered for 30 minutes.

2. Thread the shrimp onto 8 metal or wooden skewers. Preheat the grill for 8 minutes before use. Place on greased grill rack. Cook, covered, over medium heat until shrimp turns pink, 5-6 minutes, turning once. Serve with remaining pesto.

Nutrition Facts Per Serving

Calories 238, Total Fat 18g, Total Carbs 3g, Total Protein 16g

Sweet Sriracha Wings

(Prepping time: 20 minutes| Cooking time:15-20 minutes |For 12 servings)

Ingredients

- 1 tablespoon canola oil
- 2 teaspoons ground coriander
- 12 chicken wings (about 3 pounds)
- 1/2 teaspoon garlic salt
- 1/4 teaspoon pepper

Sauce:

- 1/4 cup butter, cubed
- 1/2 cup orange juice
- 1/3 cup Sriracha chili sauce
- 3 tablespoons honey
- 2 tablespoons lime juice
- 1/4 cup chopped fresh cilantro

Directions

1. Place chicken wings in a large bowl. Mix oil, garlic salt, coriander, and pepper; add to wings and toss to coat. Refrigerate, covered, 2 hours or overnight.

2. For making the sauce, melt butter in a small saucepan. Stir in orange juice, chili sauce, honey, and lime juice until blended.

3. Preheat the grill for 8 minutes before grilling anything in it. Grill wings while covered over medium heat 15-18 minutes or until juices run clear, turning occasionally; brush with some of the sauce during the last 5 minutes of grilling.

4. Transfer chicken to a large bowl; add remaining sauce and toss to coat. Sprinkle with cilantro.

Nutrition Facts Per Serving

Calories 197, Total Fat 13g, Total Carbs 8g, Total Protein 12g

Grilled Beef-Mushroom Burgers

(Prepping time: 10 minutes| Cooking time:10 minutes |For 4 servings)

Ingredients

- 4 ounces sliced button mushrooms
- 3/4 teaspoon kosher salt, divided
- 1/3 cup chopped cucumber
- 1/4 cup plain whole-milk Greek yogurt
- 1 pound 90% lean ground sirloin
- 2 tablespoons olive oil
- 1/8 teaspoon black pepper
- 2 tablespoons minced roasted garlic (about 4 large cloves)
- 1 tablespoon fresh lemon juice
- 4 heirloom tomato slices
- 1 tablespoon chopped fresh flat-leaf parsley
- 8 large butter lettuce leaves
- 4 red onion slices

Directions

1. Preheat the grill for 8 minutes before use. Place the mushrooms in a food processor and process until minced, about 1 minute.

2. Mix mushrooms, ground sirloin, oil, pepper, and 3/8 teaspoon salt in a medium bowl; gently shape into 4 (4-inch) patties and place on a baking sheet lined with parchment paper.

3. Mix together cucumber, yogurt, garlic, lemon juice, parsley, and remaining 3/8 teaspoon salt in a small bowl; set aside.

4. Place the burgers on grill and grill while uncovered to the desired degree of doneness, about 4 minutes per side for medium.

5. Put two lettuce leaves on each plate and top each with a burger patty, tomato slice, red onion slice, and 1 heaping tablespoon yogurt mixture.

Nutrition Facts Per Serving

Calories 303, Total Fat 19g, Total Carbs 7g, Total Protein 26g

Sun-Dried Tomato Turkey Burgers

(Prepping time: 10 minutes| Cooking time:15 minutes |For 6 servings)

Ingredients

- 2/3 cup chopped oil-packed sun-dried tomatoes
- 1/4 teaspoon salt
- 1 large red onion
- 1 cup (4 ounces) crumbled feta cheese, divided
- 1/4 teaspoon pepper
- 6 ciabatta rolls, split
- 2 pounds lean ground turkey

Directions

1. Cut the onion in half. Thinly slice the first half and finely chop the other half. Combine 1/2 cup feta, sun-dried tomatoes, chopped onion, salt, and pepper in a large bowl. Crumble turkey over mixture and mix well. Shape into six patties.

2. Preheat the grill for 8 minutes before use. Grill burgers while covered over medium heat, or broil 4 in. Away from the heat for 6 to 7 minutes on each side or until the temperature reads 165°F and juices run clear.

3. Meanwhile, in a small nonstick skillet coated with cooking spray, saute sliced onion until tender. Serve burgers on buns with onion and remaining feta.

Nutrition Facts Per Serving

Calories 1106, Total Fat 46g, Total Carbs 116g, Total Protein 57g

Grilled Sausage-Basil Pizzas

(Prepping time: 10 minutes| Cooking time: 20-25 minutes |For 4 servings)

Ingredients

- 1/4 cup olive oil
- 1 cup tomato basil pasta sauce
- 4 Italian sausage links (4 ounces each)
- 4 naan flatbreads or whole pita bread
- 2 cups shredded part-skim mozzarella cheese
- 1/2 cup thinly sliced fresh basil
- 1/2 cup grated Parmesan cheese

Directions

1. Preheat the grill for 8 minutes before using it.

2. Grill sausages while covered over medium heat until the temperature reads 160°F, 10-12 minutes, turning occasionally. Cut into 1/4-in. Slices.

3. Brush both sides of flatbreads with oil. Grill flatbreads while covered over medium heat until bottoms are lightly browned, 2-3 minutes.

4. Remove from grill and layer grilled sides with sauce, sausage, cheeses, and basil. Return to grill; cook while covered, until cheese is melted, 2-3 minutes longer.

Nutrition Facts Per Serving

Calories 804, Total Fat 56g, Total Carbs 41g, Total Protein 34g

Chapter 3: Chicken and Poultry Recipes

Turkey Tomato Burgers

(Prepping time: 5-10 minutes| Cooking time:40 minutes |For 4 servings)

Ingredients

- 6 burger bums sliced
- 1 large red onion, chopped
- ¼ teaspoon pepper
- 2 pounds turkey, lean and ground
- 1 cup feta, crumbled
- ¼ teaspoon salt
- 2/3 cup sun-dried tomatoes, chopped

Directions

1. In a mixing bowl, add all the ingredients. Combine the ingredients to mix well with each other.

2. Prepare six patties from the mixture.

3. Take Ninja Foodi Grill, arrange it over your kitchen platform, and open the top lid.

4. Arrange the grill grate and close the top lid.

5. Press "GRILL" and select the "MED" grill function. Adjust the timer to 14 minutes and then press "START/STOP." Ninja Foodi will start pre-heating.

6. Ninja Foodi is pre-heated and ready to cook when it starts to beep. After you hear a beep, open the top lid.

7. Arrange your patties over the grill grate

8. Lock lid and cook for 7 minutes, flip the patties and cook for 7 minutes more

9. Serve with ciabatta rolls with topping such as ketchup, cheese, etc.

Nutrition Facts Per Serving

Calories: 305, Fat: 17 g, Saturated Fat: 5 g, Carbohydrates: 8 g, Fiber: 2 g, Sodium: 580 mg, Protein: 31 g

Spice Lover's Hot Pepper Wings

(Prepping time: 5-10 minutes| Cooking time: 25 minutes |For 4 servings)

Ingredients

- 1-pound chicken wings
- ½ cup hot pepper sauce
- 2 tablespoons butter, melted
- ½ teaspoon paprika
- 1 tablespoon ranch salad dressing
- 1 tablespoon coconut oil

Directions

1. Take your chicken into a bowl
2. Add oil, chicken, ranch dressing, paprika
3. Mix them well
4. Let it chill for 30-60 minutes
5. Add pepper sauce and butter into another bowl
6. Pre-heat Ninja Foodi by pressing the "GRILL" option and setting it to "MED."
7. Set the timer to 25 minutes
8. Let it pre-heat until you hear a beep
9. Arrange chicken wings over the grill grate
10. Lock lid and cook for 25 minutes
11. Serve immediately with pepper sauce
12. Enjoy!

Nutrition Facts Per Serving

Calories: 510, Fat: 24 g, Saturated Fat: 7 g, Carbohydrates: 6 g, Fiber: 0.5 g, Sodium: 841 mg, Protein: 54 g

Chicken Alfredo Apples Delight

(Prepping time: 5-10 minutes| Cooking time:20 minutes |For 4 servings)

Ingredients

- 4 chicken breasts, halved
- ¼ cup blue cheese, crumbled
- 1 large apple, wedged
- 4 teaspoons chicken seasoning
- 4 slices provolone cheese
- ½ cup alfredo sauce
- 1 tablespoon lemon juice

Directions

1. Add chicken in a bowl and season with all the listed seasoning
2. Add apple and lemon juice into another bowl
3. Toss them well
4. Pre-heat Ninja Foodi by pressing the "GRILL" option and setting it to "MED."
5. Set the timer to 16 minutes
6. Let it pre-heat until you hear a beep
7. Arrange chicken over Grill Grate and lock lid
8. Cook for 8 minutes and flip the chicken
9. Grill for 8 minutes more and then remove it
10. Once done, grill an apple for 2 minutes
11. Serve chicken with apple, blue cheese, and alfredo sauce
12. Enjoy!

Nutrition Facts Per Serving

Calories: 247, Fat: 19 g, Saturated Fat: 3 g, Carbohydrates: 29 g, Fiber: 2 g, Sodium: 850 mg, Protein: 14 g

Mesmerizing Alfredo Apple Chicken

(Prepping time: 5-10 minutes| Cooking time:20 minutes |For 4 servings)

Ingredients

- ½ cup alfredo sauce
- ¼ cup blue cheese, crumbled
- 4 slices provolone cheese
- 4 teaspoons chicken seasoning
- 4 chicken breast, halved
- 1 tablespoon lemon juice
- 1 large apple, wedged

Directions

1. Take a medium-sized bowl and add chicken breasts, season them well
2. Take another bowl and add lemon juice, apple
3. Pre-heat your Ninja Foodi in "GRILL" mode on the "MED" settings, setting the timer to 20 minutes
4. Once you hear the beep, arrange the prepared chicken over the grill grate
5. Cook for 8 minutes, flip and cook for 8 minutes more, remove the chicken
6. Grill marinated apples in the same process, 2 minutes per side
7. Serve the prepared chicken dish with alfredo sauce, blue cheese, pepper, and apple
8. Have fun!

Nutrition Facts Per Serving

Calories: 247, Fat: 19 g, Saturated Fat: 6 g, Carbohydrates: 29 g, Fiber: 6 g, Sodium: 853 mg, Protein: 14 g

Juicy BBQ Chicken

(Prepping time: 5-10 minutes| Cooking time:12 minutes |For 4 servings)

Ingredients

- 6 chicken drumsticks
- ½ tablespoon Worcestershire sauce
- 2 teaspoons BBQ seasoning
- 1 tablespoon brown sugar
- 1 teaspoon dried onion, chopped
- 1/3 cup spice seasoning
- 1 tablespoon bourbon
- 1 pinch teaspoon salt
- ½ cup ketchup

Directions

1. Add all ingredients into a saucepan except drumsticks
2. Stir cook for 8-10 minutes
3. Keep them aside and let it cool
4. Pre-heat Ninja Foodi by pressing the "GRILL" option and setting it to "MED."
5. Set the timer to 12 minutes
6. Let it pre-heat until you hear a beep
7. Arrange drumsticks over grill grate, brush with remaining sauce
8. Lock lid and cook for 6 minutes
9. flip and brush with more sauce
10. Cook for 6 minutes more
11. Serve and enjoy!

Nutrition Facts Per Serving

Calories: 300, Fat: 8 g, Saturated Fat: 1 g, Carbohydrates: 10 g, Fiber: 1.5 g, Sodium: 319 mg, Protein: 12.5 g

Orange Grilled Chicken Meal

(Prepping time: 5-10 minutes| Cooking time:15 minutes |For 4 servings)

Ingredients

- 12 chicken wings
- 2 tablespoons lime juice
- ¼ cup cilantro, chopped
- 2 teaspoons coriander, grounded
- 1 tablespoon canola oil
- 1/3 cup Sriracha chili sauce
- ¼ cup butter, melted
- 3 tablespoons honey
- ½ cup of orange juice
- ½ teaspoon garlic salt
- ¼ teaspoon ground black pepper

Directions

1. Coat the chicken with oil, season with spices
2. Let it chill for 2 hours
3. Add listed ingredients and keep it on the side
4. Cook for 3-4 minutes in a saucepan
5. Pre-heat your Ninja Foodi by pressing the "GRILL" option and setting it to "MED."
6. Set your timer to 10 minutes
7. Let it pre-heat until it beeps
8. Arrange chicken over grill grate, cook for 5 minutes
9. Flip and let it cook for 5 minutes more
10. Serve with sauce on top
11. Serve and enjoy!

Nutrition Facts Per Serving

Calories: 320, Fat: 14 g, Saturated Fat: 4 g, Carbohydrates: 19 g, Fiber: 1 g, Sodium: 258 mg, Protein: 25 g

Juicy Moroccan Chicken Roast

(Prepping time: 5-10 minutes| Cooking time:22 minutes |For 4 servings)

Ingredients

- ¼ teaspoon red pepper flakes, crushed
- 2 teaspoons paprika
- 2 teaspoons cumin, ground
- ½ teaspoon fresh flat-leaf parsley, chopped
- 1/3 cup olive oil
- ½ teaspoon salt
- 4 garlic cloves, chopped
- 4 skinless, boneless chicken thighs
- 3 tablespoons plain yogurt

Directions

1. Add garlic, yogurt, salt, oil to your food processor and blend well

2. Take a mixing bowl and add red pepper flakes, chicken, paprika, cumin, parsley, garlic and mix

3. Let the chicken marinate for about 2-4 hours

4. Pre-heat your Ninja Foodi In "ROAST" mode, setting the temperature to "400 degrees F" and the time to 23 minutes

5. Once you hear the beep, arrange the chicken directly in the cooking pot

6. Let them cook for 15 minutes, flip and cook until the timer hits zero

7. Serve and enjoy once done!

Nutrition Facts Per Serving

Calories: 321, Fat: 24 g, Saturated Fat: 5 g, Carbohydrates: 6 g, Fiber: 2 g, Sodium: 602 mg, Protein: 21 g

Orange Flavored Chicken Delight

(Prepping time: 5-10 minutes| Cooking time:15 minutes |For 4 servings)

Ingredients

- 2 teaspoons ground coriander
- ½ teaspoon garlic salt
- ¼ teaspoon ground black pepper
- 12 chicken wings
- 1 tablespoon canola oil
- ¼ cup butter, melted
- 3 tablespoons honey
- ½ cup of orange juice
- 1/3 cup Sriracha chili sauce
- 2 tablespoons lime juice
- ¼ cup cilantro, chopped

Directions

1. Take your chicken into a bowl
2. Add oil, chicken, ranch dressing, paprika
3. Mix them well
4. Let it chill for 30-60 minutes
5. Add pepper sauce and butter into another bowl
6. Pre-heat Ninja Foodi by pressing the "GRILL" option and setting it to "MED."
7. Set the timer to 25 minutes
8. Let it pre-heat until you hear a beep
9. Arrange chicken wings over the grill grate
10. Lock lid and cook for 25 minutes
11. Serve immediately with pepper sauce
12. Enjoy!

Nutrition Facts Per Serving

Calories: 510, Fat: 24 g, Saturated Fat: 7 g, Carbohydrates: 6 g, Fiber: 0.5 g, Sodium: 841 mg, Protein: 54 g

Fancy Turkey Bacon Roast

(Prepping time: 5-10 minutes| Cooking time:20 minutes |For 6 servings)

Ingredients

- 8 pieces (6 ounces each) turkey cutlets
- 8 ham slices
- 4 tablespoons sage leaves
- 2 tablespoons butter, melted
- Pepper and salt to taste

Directions

1. Take your turkey cutlets into a bowl and season with salt and pepper
2. Wrap them with bacon
3. Brush with butter and add sage leaves on top
4. Take your baking pan and generously grease with butter
5. Pre-heat Ninja Foodi by pressing the "BAKE" option and setting it to "350-degree F."
6. Set the timer to 20 minutes
7. Let it pre-heat until you hear a beep
8. Arrange cutlets in a baking pan and transfer to Grill
9. Cook for 20 minutes
10. Serve and enjoy!

Nutrition Facts Per Serving

Calories: 450, Fat: 20 g, Saturated Fat: 4 g, Carbohydrates: 2 g, Fiber: 0.5 g, Sodium: 656 mg, Protein: 51 g

Juicy Moroccan Chicken Roast

(Prepping time: 5-10 minutes| Cooking time:22 minutes |For 4 servings)

Ingredients

- 4 skinless, boneless chicken thighs
- 3 tablespoons plain yogurt
- 2 teaspoons paprika
- ½ teaspoon fresh flat-leaf parsley, chopped
- 1/3 cup olive oil
- 2 teaspoons cumin, ground
- 4 garlic cloves, chopped
- ½ teaspoon salt
- ¼ teaspoon red pepper flakes, crushed

Directions

1. Add garlic, yogurt, salt, oil to your food processor
2. Blend them well
3. Add chicken, paprika, cumin, red pepper flakes, parsley, garlic into a mixing bowl
4. Mix them well
5. Let the chicken marinate for about 2-4 hours
6. Pre-heat your Ninja Foodi In "ROAST" mode, setting the temperature to "400 degrees F."
7. Set the timer to 23 minutes
8. Once you hear the beep, arrange the chicken directly in the cooking pot
9. Let them cook for 15 minutes
10. Then flip and cook for 8 minutes
11. Serve and enjoy!

Nutrition Facts Per Serving

Calories: 321, Fat: 24 g, Saturated Fat: 5 g, Carbohydrates: 6 g, Fiber: 2 g, Sodium: 602 mg, Protein: 21 g

Turkey Burger with Tomato Dress

(Prepping time: 10 minutes | Cooking time: 40 minutes | For 4 servings)

Ingredients

- 2 pounds lean turkey, grounded
- 6 burger buns of your choice, sliced in half
- 1 cup feta cheese, crumbled
- 3 ounces plain granola
- 2/3 cup sun-dried tomatoes, chopped
- 1 large red onion, chopped
- ¼ teaspoon salt
- ¼ teaspoon pepper

Directions

1. Add all the ingredients into a mixing bowl
2. Combine them well
3. Arrange the grill grate
4. Close the lid
5. Pre-heat Ninja Foodi by pressing the "GRILL" option and setting it to "MED."
6. Set the timer to 14 minutes
7. Let it pre-heat until you hear a beep
8. Arrange the patties over the grill grate and lock lid
9. Cook for 7 minutes more
10. Serve warm with ciabatta rolls
11. Enjoy!

Nutrition Facts Per Serving

Calories: 298, Fat: 16 g, Saturated Fat: 4 g, Carbohydrates: 32 g, Fiber: 4 g, Sodium: 168 mg, Protein: 27

Chapter 4: Pork and Other Meat Recipes

Bourbon-y Pork Chops

(Prepping time: 5-10 minutes| Cooking time: 20 minutes |For 5 servings)

Ingredients

- ½ tablespoon dry mustard powder
- 1 cup brown sugar, packed
- ¾ cup bourbon
- 2 cups ketchup
- 3 tablespoons Worcestershire sauce
- ¼ cup of soy sauce
- ¼ cup apple cider vinegar
- Salt and pepper to taste
- 4 boneless pork chops

Directions

1. Take your Grill and set it to "MED" mode and timer to 15 minutes
2. Once you hear a beep, transfer the pork chops over your grill grate
3. Cook for 8 minutes, flip them over and cook for the remaining time until cooked
4. Take a saucepan and place it over medium heat, add remaining ingredients and heat them
5. Bring the sauce to a boil and lower heat, simmer for 20 minutes
6. Drizzle the sauce over pork
7. Enjoy!

Nutrition Facts Per Serving

Calories: 346, Fat: 13 g, Saturated Fat: 4 g, Carbohydrates: 27 g, Fiber: 0.4 g, Sodium: 1324 mg, Protein: 27 g

Lovely American Grilled Burger

(Prepping time: 10 minutes| Cooking time: 20 minutes |For 4 servings)

Ingredients

- 1 tablespoon olive oil
- 1-pound ground beef
- 4 seed hamburger buns, cut in half
- ½ teaspoon salt
- 1 large egg, whisked
- ½ teaspoon pepper
- ½ cup breadcrumbs

Directions

1. Take a medium-sized bowl and add listed ingredients, except oil and buns
2. Mix well and make about 4 patties out of the mixture
3. Brush the patties with olive oil
4. Pre-heat your Ninja Food Grill to HIGH setting, set a timer to 10 minutes
5. Once beeping sound is heard, transfer 2 patties to Grill and cook for 5 minutes per side
6. Grill remaining patties in a similar manner
7. Serve with the buns
8. Enjoy!

Nutrition Facts Per Serving

Calories: 301, Fat: 15 g, Saturated Fat: 3 g, Carbohydrates: 11 g, Fiber: 0.3 g, Sodium: 398 mg, Protein: 28 g

Simple Coffee Flavored Steak

(Prepping time: 10 minutes| Cooking time: 50 minutes |For 4 servings)

Ingredients

- 1 and ½ pounds beef flank steak
- 1 teaspoon instant espresso powder
- ½ teaspoon garlic powder
- 2 teaspoons chili powder
- 2 tablespoons olive oil
- Salt and pepper, to taste

Directions

1. Insert the grill grate and close the hood
2. Pre-heat Ninja Foodi by pressing the "GRILL" option at and setting it to "HIGH" and timer to 40 minutes
3. Once it pre-heat until you hear a beep
4. Make the dry rub by mixing the chili powder, espresso powder, garlic powder, salt, and pepper
5. Rub all over the steak and brush with oil
6. Place on the grill grate and cook for 40 minutes
7. Flip after 20 minutes
8. Serve and enjoy!

Nutrition Facts Per Serving

Calories: 250, Fat: 14 g, Saturated Fat: 4 g, Carbohydrates: 6 g, Fiber: 2 g, Sodium: 294 mg, Protein: 20 g

Delish Pineapple Steak

(Prepping time: 5-10 minutes| Cooking time:8 minutes |For 4 servings)

Ingredients

- Chili powder as needed
- ¼ cup cilantro leaves, chopped
- 1 tablespoon lime juice
- Salt and pepper to taste
- 1 tablespoon canola oil
- 4 fillet mignon steaks, 6-8 ounces
- 1 medium red onion, diced
- 1 jalapeno seeded and stemmed, diced
- ½ medium pineapple, cored and diced

Directions

1. Take your fillets and rub them generously with salt and pepper
2. Pre-heat your Ninja Foodi Grill to HIGH, set a timer to 8 minutes
3. Once you hear the beep, transfer your prepared meat to the Grill Grate
4. Cook until the internal temperature reaches 125 degrees F
5. Take a bowl and add pineapple, jalapeno, onion, and mix
6. Add lime juice, chili powder, coriander
7. Serve the prepared fillets with the mixture with pineapple on top
8. Enjoy!

Nutrition Facts Per Serving

Calories: 530, Fat: 22 g, Saturated Fat: 7 g, Carbohydrates: 21 g, Fiber: 4 g, Sodium: 286 mg, Protein: 58 g

Authentic Korean Flank Steak

(Prepping time: 10 minutes| Cooking time:1 minute |For 4 servings)

Ingredients

- 1 teaspoon red pepper flakes
- ½ cup and 1 tablespoon soy sauce
- 1 and ½ pounds flank steak
- ¼ cup and 2 tablespoon vegetable oil
- ½ cup of rice wine vinegar
- 3 tablespoons sriracha
- 2 cucumbers, seeded and sliced
- 4 garlic cloves, minced
- 2 tablespoons ginger, minced
- 2 tablespoons honey
- 3 tablespoons sesame oil
- 1 teaspoon sugar
- Salt to taste

Directions

1. Take a bowl and add ½ cup soy sauce, half of rice wine, honey, ginger,r garlic, 2 tablespoons sriracha, 2 tablespoons sesame oil, vegetable oil

2. Mix well, pour half of the mixture over steak and rub well

3. Cover steak and let it sit for 10 minutes

4. Prepare the salad mix by add remaining rice wine vinegar, sesame oil, sugar red pepper flakes, sriracha sauce, soy sauce and salt in a salad bowl

5. Pre-heat your Ninja Foodi Grill on HIGH setting, with the timer set to 12 minutes

6. Transfer steak to your Grill and cook for 6 minutes per side

7. Slice and serve with the salad mix

8. Enjoy!

Nutrition Facts Per Serving

Calories: 327, Fat: 4 g, Saturated Fat: 0.5 g, Carbohydrates: 33 g, Fiber: 1 g, Sodium: 142 mg, Protein: 24 g

The Yogurt Lamb Skewers

(Prepping time: 10 minutes| Cooking time: 16 minutes |For 4 servings)

Ingredients

- 2 garlic clove, minced
- 1 pack of 10 ounces couscous
- 1 tablespoon and 1 teaspoon cumin
- 2 lemons, juiced
- 1 and ½ cup of yogurt
- Salt to taste
- 1 and ½ pound lamb leg, boneless, cubed
- Fresh ground black pepper
- 2 tomatoes, seeded and diced
- ½ small red onion, chopped
- 3 tablespoons olive oil
- ½ cucumber, seeded and diced
- ¼ cup finely chopped fresh parsley
- ¼ cup fresh mint, chopped
- Lemon wedges to serve

Directions

1. Cook couscous following the package Directionsand fluffy t up with a fork
2. Whisk yogurt with garlic, cumin, lemon juice, salt, pepper in a large-sized bowl
3. Add lamb, mix well to coat it
4. Separate toss red onion, cucumber, tomatoes, parsley, mint, lemon juice, olive oil, salt and couscous in a salad bowl
5. Thread your seasoned lamb on 8 skewers and drizzle salt and pepper over them
6. Pre-heat your Ninja Foodi Grill on HIGH, set timer to 16 minutes
7. Once you hear the beep, place 4 skewers on the grill
8. Let it cook for 4 minutes per side
9. Cook the remaining ones in a similar way
10. Serve and enjoy!

Nutrition Facts Per Serving

Calories: 417, Fat: 11 g, Saturated Fat: 5 g, Carbohydrates: 20 g, Fiber: 2 g, Sodium: 749 mg, Protein: 13 g

Generous Pesto Beef Meal

(Prepping time: 10 minutes| Cooking time: 14 minutes |For 4 servings)

Ingredients

- ½ teaspoon pepper
- ½ teaspoon salt
- ½ cup feta cheese, crumbled
- 2/3 cup pesto
- ½ cup walnuts, chopped
- 4 cups grape tomatoes, halved
- 4 cups penne pasta, uncooked
- 10 ounces baby spinach, chopped
- 4 beef (6 ounces each) tenderloin steaks

Directions

1. Cook the pasta according to the package Directions
2. Drain the pasta and rinse it
3. Keep the pasta on the side
4. Season the tenderloin steaks with pepper and salt
5. Pre-heat your Ninja Foodi Grill to HIGH and set the timer to 7 minutes
6. You will hear a beep once the pre-heating sequence is complete
7. Transfer steak to your grill and cook for 7 minutes, flip and cook for 7 minutes more
8. Take a bowl and add pasta, walnuts, spinach, tomatoes, and pesto
9. Mix well
10. Garnish your steak with cheese and serve with the prepared sauce
11. Enjoy!

Nutrition Facts Per Serving

Calories: 361, Fat: 5 g, Saturated Fat: 1 g, Carbohydrates: 16 g, Fiber: 4 g, Sodium: 269 mg, Protein: 33 g

Cool Avocado Steak Salad

(Prepping time: 5-10 minutes| Cooking time:18 minutes |For 4 servings)

Ingredients

- 1 cup cilantro leaves
- 2 ripe avocados, diced
- 2 cups salsa Verde
- 2 beef lank steak, diced
- ½ teaspoon salt
- ½ teaspoon pepper
- 2 medium tomatoes, seeded and diced

Directions

1. Take your beefsteak and season them generously with salt and pepper
2. Pre-heat your Ninja Food Grill in MED temperature, setting the time to 18 minutes
3. Once you hear the beep, arrange your diced steak over the grill grate
4. Cook for 9 minutes, flip them and cook for 9 minutes more
5. Take your blender and add salsa, cilantro until you have a fine mixture
6. Serve your steak with the salsa, avocado, and tomato
7. Enjoy the whole meal!

Nutrition Facts Per Serving

Calories: 520, Fat: 31 g, Saturated Fat: 9 g, Carbohydrates: 38 g, Fiber: 2 g, Sodium: 301 mg, Protein: 41 g

Italian Basil Pizza

(Prepping time: 10 minutes| Cooking time: 17 minutes |For 4 servings)

Ingredients

- 4 pieces (4 ounces each) sausage, sliced
- 1 cup tomato basil pasta
- ½ cup parmesan cheese, grated
- 4 flat pieces of bread
- ¼ cup olive oil
- 2 cups mozzarella cheese, shredded
- ½ cup fresh basil, thinly sliced

Directions

1. Pre-heat your Ninja Foodi Grill on HIGH settings, setting a timer to 12minutes
2. Once you hear the beep, transfer sausage slices to grill
3. Grill for 3 minutes per side
4. Similarly, grill flatbreads for 3 minutes per side (making sure to oil them first)
5. Top your grilled bread with sausage, basil, cheese, and sauce
6. Place bread in grill and cook on BAKE mode for 5 minutes on LOW settings
7. Slice and serve
8. Enjoy!

Nutrition Facts Per Serving

Calories: 308, Fat: 20 g, Saturated Fat: 3 g, Carbohydrates: 40 g, Fiber: 4 g, Sodium: 688 mg, Protein: 49 g

Juicy Korean Chii Pork Delight

(Prepping time: 5-10 minutes| Cooking time:8 minutes |For 4 servings)

Ingredients

- Red pepper flakes
- 3 teaspoons pepper
- 2 tablespoon sesame seeds
- 3 tablespoons Korean Red Chili Paste
- ½ cup brown sugar
- ½ cup of soy sauce
- 1 yellow onion, sliced
- 3 tablespoons green onion, minced
- 5 garlic cloves, minced
- 2 pounds pork, cut into 1/8 inch slices

Directions

1. Take a re-sealable zip bag and add all of the listed ingredients
2. Zip up the bag and let it sit in your fridge for 6-8 hours
3. Pre-heat your Ninja Foodi Grill in MED heat setting timer to 8 minutes
4. Arrange the sliced-up pork over your grill grate
5. Lock lid and cook for 4 minutes, flip the meat and cook for 4 minutes more
6. Serve with chopped lettuce
7. Enjoy!

Nutrition Facts Per Serving

Calories: 621, Fat: 31 g, Saturated Fat: 12 g, Carbohydrates: 29 g, Fiber: 3 g, Sodium: 1428 mg, Protein: 53 g

Chapter 5: Fish and Seafood Recipes

Salmon and Dill Sauce Meal

(Prepping time: 10 minutes| Cooking time:20-25 minutes |For 4 servings)

Ingredients

- 4 salmon, each of 6 ounces
- 2 teaspoons olive oil
- 1 pinch salt

Dill Sauce

- ½ cup non-fat Greek Yogurt
- ½ cup sour cream
- Pinch of salt
- 2 tablespoons dill, chopped

Directions

1. Pre-heat Ninja Foodi by pressing the "AIR CRISP" option and setting it to "270 Degrees F" and timer to 25 minutes

2. Wait until the appliance beeps

3. Drizzle cut pieces of salmon with 1 teaspoon olive oil

4. Season with salt

5. Take the cooking basket out and transfer salmon to basket, cook for 20-23 minutes

6. Take a bowl and add sour cream, salt, chopped dill, yogurt and mix well to prepare the dill sauce

7. Serve cooked salmon by pouring the sauce all over

8. Garnish with chopped dill and enjoy!

Nutrition Facts Per Serving

Calories: 600, Fat: 45 g, Saturated Fat: 6 g, Carbohydrates: 5 g, Fiber: 2 g, Sodium: 422 mg, Protein: 60 g

Freshly Baked Haddock

(Prepping time: 5-10 minutes| Cooking time:13 minutes |For 3 servings)

Ingredients

- 1-pound haddock fillets
- ¾ cup breadcrumbs
- ¼ cup parmesan cheese, grated
- ¼ teaspoon ground dried thyme
- ¼ cup butter, melted
- ¾ cup milk
- ¼ teaspoon salt

Directions

1. Coat fish fillets in milk, then season with salt
2. Keep it on the side
3. Add breadcrumbs, parmesan, cheese, thyme into a mixing bowl
4. Combine them well
5. Coat fillets in bread crumb mixture
6. Pre-heat Ninja Foodi by pressing the "BAKE" option and setting it to "325 Degrees F."
7. Set the timer to 13 minutes
8. Let it pre-heat until you hear a beep
9. Arrange fish fillets directly over Grill Grate and lock lid
10. Cook for 8 minutes
11. Flip and cook for 5 minutes
12. Serve and enjoy!

Nutrition Facts Per Serving

Calories: 450, Fat: 27 g, Saturated Fat: 12 g, Carbohydrates: 16 g, Fiber: 22 g, Sodium: 1056 mg, Protein: 44 g

Italian Garlic Salmon

(Prepping time: 5-10 minutes| Cooking time:12 minutes |For 3 servings)

Ingredients

- 2 salmon fillets, 6 ounces each
- 1 garlic clove, minced
- 1 teaspoon lemon zest, grated
- ¼ teaspoon fresh rosemary, minced
- ¼ teaspoon salt
- ¼ teaspoon pepper

Directions

1. Add all listed ingredients except salmon into a mixing bowl
2. Mix them well
3. Add salmon and combine thoroughly
4. Keep it aside for 15 minutes
5. Pre-heat Ninja Foodi by pressing the "GRILL" option and setting it to "MED."
6. Set the timer to 6 minutes
7. Let it pre-heat until you hear a beep
8. Arrange salmon over the grill grate
9. Lock lid and cook for 3 minutes
10. Flip and cook for 3 minutes more
11. Serve and enjoy!

Nutrition Facts Per Serving

Calories: 250, Fat: 8 g, Saturated Fat: 3g, Carbohydrates: 22 g, Fiber: 3 g, Sodium: 370 mg, Protein: 36 g

Daring Spicy Grilled Shrimp

(Prepping time: 5-10 minutes| Cooking time: 6 minutes |For 4 servings)

Ingredients

- 1 teaspoon garlic salt
- ½ teaspoon black pepper
- 1 tablespoon paprika
- 1 tablespoon garlic powder
- 2 tablespoons olive oil
- 1-pound jumbo shrimps, peeled and deveined
- 2 tablespoons brown sugar

Directions

1. Take a mixing bowl and add listed ingredients to mix well

2. Let it chill and marinate for 30-60 minutes

3. Preheat Ninja Foodi by pressing the "GRILL" option and setting it to "MED" and timer to 6 minutes

4. Let it preheat until you hear a beep

5. Arrange prepared shrimps over grill grate, lock lid and cook for 3 minutes, flip and cook for 3 minutes more

6. Serve and enjoy!

Nutrition Facts Per Serving

Calories: 370, Fat: 27 g, Saturated Fat: 3 g, Carbohydrates: 23 g, Fiber: 8 g, Sodium: 182 mg, Protein: 6 g

Paprika Grilled Shrimp

(Prepping time: 5-10 minutes| Cooking time: 6 minutes |For 4 servings)

Ingredients

- 1-pound jumbo shrimps, peeled and deveined
- 2 tablespoons brown sugar
- 1 tablespoon paprika
- 1 tablespoon garlic powder
- 2 tablespoons olive oil
- 1 teaspoon garlic salt
- ½ teaspoon black pepper

Directions

1. Add listed ingredients into a mixing bowl
2. Mix them well
3. Let it chill and marinate for 30-60 minutes
4. Pre-heat Ninja Foodi by pressing the "GRILL" option and setting it to "MED."
5. Set the timer to 6 minutes
6. Let it pre-heat until you hear a beep
7. Arrange prepared shrimps over the grill grate
8. Lock lid and cook for 3 minutes
9. Then flip and cook for 3 minutes more
10. Serve and enjoy!

Nutrition Facts Per Serving

Calories: 370, Fat: 27 g, Saturated Fat: 3 g, Carbohydrates: 23 g, Fiber: 8 g, Sodium: 182 mg, Protein: 6 g

Subtly Roasted BBQ Shrimp

(Prepping time: 5-10 minutes| Cooking time:7 minutes |For 2 servings)

Ingredients

- 3 tablespoons chipotle in adobo sauce, minced
- ¼ teaspoon salt
- ¼ cup BBQ sauce
- ½ orange, juiced
- ½ pound large shrimps

Directions

7. Take a mixing bowl and add all ingredients, mix well

8. Keep it on the side

9. Pre-heat Ninja Foodi by pressing the "ROAST" option and setting it to "400 Degrees F" and timer to 7 minutes

10. Let it pre-heat until you hear a beep

11. Arrange shrimps over Grill Grate and lock lid, cook until the timer runs out

12. Serve and enjoy!

Nutrition Facts Per Serving

Calories: 173, Fat: 2 g, Saturated Fat: 0.5 g, Carbohydrates: 21 g, Fiber: 2 g, Sodium: 1143 mg, Protein: 17 g

Coho Glazed Salmon

(Prepping time: 10 minutes| Cooking time: 25 minutes |For 4 servings)

Ingredients

- 1-2 coho salmon filets
- 1 cup of water
- ¼ cup of soy sauce
- ¼ cup brown sugar
- 1 tablespoon honey
- 1 and ½ tablespoons ginger roots, minced
- ½ teaspoon white pepper
- 2 tablespoons cornstarch
- ¼ cup of cold water

Directions

1. Insert the grill grate and close the hood
2. Preheat Ninja Foodi by pressing the "GRILL" option and setting it to "HIGH" for 15 minutes
3. Take a medium saucepan over medium heat, combine sauce ingredients(except salmon, cornstarch and cold water) and bring to a low boil
4. Then add cornstarch and water in another bowl, whisk cornstarch mixture slowly into sauce until it thickens
5. Add one chunk of pecan wood to the hot coal of your grill
6. Brush sauce onto the salmon filet
7. Place on the grill grate, then close the hood
8. Cook for 15 minutes
9. Brush the salmon with another coat of sauce
10. Close the lid and cook for 10 minutes more
11. Serve and enjoy!

Nutrition Facts Per Serving

Calories: 163, Fat: 0 g, Saturated Fat: 0 g, Carbohydrates: 15 g, Fiber: 3 g, Sodium: 456 mg, Protein: 0 g

Spicy Buttered Salmon

(Prepping time: 5-10 minutes| Cooking time:12 minutes |For 4 servings)

Ingredients

- 2 pounds salmon fillets
- 6 tablespoons butter, melted
- 1 and ¼ teaspoon onion salt
- 1 teaspoon dry oregano
- 2 tablespoons lemon pepper
- 1 teaspoon dry basil
- 1 teaspoon ancho chili powder
- Lemon wedges and dill sprigs
- 2 teaspoons cayenne pepper
- 2 teaspoon salt
- 1 teaspoon white pepper, ground
- 1 teaspoon black pepper, ground

Directions

1. Take a mixing bowl and add listed ingredients
2. Season salmon fillets with butter
3. Coat salmon fillets with the mixture
4. Pre-heat Ninja Foodi by pressing the "GRILL" option and setting it to "MED."
5. Set the timer to 10 minutes
6. Let it pre-heat until you hear a beep
7. Arrange prepared fillets over the grill grate
8. cook for 5 minutes
9. then flip and cook for 5 minutes more
10. Serve and enjoy!

Nutrition Facts Per Serving

Calories: 300, Fat: 8 g, Saturated Fat: 2 g, Carbohydrates: 17 g, Fiber: 1 g, Sodium: 342 mg, Protein: 26 g

Spicy Cajun Shrimp

(Prepping time: 10 minutes| Cooking time: 7 minutes |For 4 servings)

Ingredients

- 1 and ¼ pound tiger shrimp, about 16-20 pieces
- ¼ teaspoon cayenne pepper
- ½ teaspoon old bay seasoning
- ¼ teaspoon smoked paprika
- 1 pinch of salt
- 1 tablespoon olive oil

Directions

1. Pre-heat Ninja Foodi by pressing the "AIR CRISP" option and setting it to "390 Degrees F" and timer to 10 minutes
2. Take a mixing bowl and add ingredients (except shrimp), mix well
3. Dip the shrimp into spice mixture and oil
4. Transfer the prepared shrimp to your Ninja Foodi Grill cooking basket and cook for 5 minutes
5. Serve and enjoy!

Nutrition Facts Per Serving

Calories: 170, Fat: 2 g, Saturated Fat: 0.5 g, Carbohydrates: 5 g, Fiber: 2 g, Sodium: 1236 mg, Protein: 23 g

Crispy Crab Patty

(Prepping time: 5-10 minutes| Cooking time:10 minutes |For 4 servings)

Ingredients

- 12 ounces lump crabmeat
- 1 shallot, minced
- 1 egg, beaten
- 2 tablespoons almond flour
- ¼ cup mayonnaise, low carb
- 2 tablespoons Dijon mustard
- ¼ cup parsley, minced
- 1 lemon, zest
- Pepper and salt as needed

Directions

1. Add all ingredients into a mixing bowl
2. Mix them well
3. Prepare 4 meat from the mixture
4. Pre-heat Ninja Foodi by pressing the "AIR CRISP" option and setting it to "375 Degrees F."
5. Set the timer to 10 minutes
6. Let it pre-heat until you hear a beep
7. Transfer patties to cooking basket
8. Cook for 5 minutes
9. Then flip and cook for 5 minutes more
10. Serve and enjoy!

Nutrition Facts Per Serving

Calories: 177, Fat: 13 g, Saturated Fat: 2 g, Carbohydrates: 2.5 g, Fiber: 0 g, Sodium: 358 mg, Protein: 11 g

Mustard-y Crisped Up Cod

(Prepping time: 5-10 minutes| Cooking time:10 minutes |For 3 servings)

Ingredients

- 1 large whole egg
- 1 teaspoon Dijon mustard
- ½ cup bread crumbs
- 1-pound cod filets
- ¼ cup all-purpose flour
- 1 tablespoon dried parsley
- 1 teaspoon paprika
- ½ teaspoon pepper

Directions

1. Take fish fillets and slice them into 1 inch wide strips
2. Take a mixing bowl and whisk in eggs, add mustard and combine well
3. Add flour in another bowl
4. Take another bowl and add bread crumbs, dried parsley, paprika, black pepper and combine well
5. Coat strips with flour, then coat with egg mix, coat with crumbs at last
6. Preheat Ninja Foodi by pressing the "AIR CRISP" option and setting it to "390 Degrees F" and timer to 10 minutes
7. Let it preheat until you hear a beep
8. Arrange strips directly inside basket, lock lid and cook until the timer runs out
9. Serve and enjoy!

Nutrition Facts Per Serving

Calories: 200, Fat: 4 g, Saturated Fat: 1 g, Carbohydrates: 17 g, Fiber: 1 g, Sodium: 214 mg, Protein: 24 g

Easy BBQ Roast Shrimp

(Prepping time: 5-10 minutes| Cooking time: 7 minutes |For 2 servings)

Ingredients

- ½ pound shrimps, large
- 3 tablespoons chipotle in adobo sauce, minced
- ½ orange, juiced
- ¼ cup BBQ sauce
- ¼ teaspoon salt

Directions

1. Add listed ingredients into a mixing bowl
2. Mix them well
3. Keep it aside
4. Pre-heat Ninja Foodi by pressing the "ROAST" option and setting it to "400 Degrees F."
5. Set the timer to 7 minutes
6. Let it pre-heat until you hear a beep
7. Arrange shrimps over Grill Grate and lock lid
8. cook for 7 minutes
9. Serve and enjoy!

Nutrition Facts Per Serving

Calories: 173, Fat: 2 g, Saturated Fat: 0.5 g, Carbohydrates: 21 g, Fiber: 2 g, Sodium: 1143 mg, Protein: 17 g

Swordfish with Caper Sauce

(Prepping time: 10 minutes| Cooking time:8 minutes |For 4 servings)

Ingredients

- 4 swordfish steaks, about 1-inch thick
- 4 tablespoons unsalted butter
- 1 lemon, sliced into 8 slices
- 1 tablespoon lemon juice
- 1 tablespoon extra-virgin olive oil
- 2 tablespoons capers, drained
- Sea salt
- Black pepper, freshly grounded

Directions

1. Take a large shallow bowl and whisk together the lemon juice and oil
2. Season with swordfish steaks with salt and pepper on each side, place in the oil mixture
3. Turn to coat both sides and refrigerate for 15 minutes
4. Insert the grill grate and close the hood
5. Preheat Ninja Foodi by pressing the "GRILL" option at and setting it to "MAX" and timer to 8 minutes
6. Let it preheat until you hear a beep
7. Arrange the swordfish over the grill grate, lock lid and cook for 9 minutes
8. Place a medium saucepan over medium heat and melt butter
9. Add the lemon slices and capers to the pan and cook for 1 minute
10. Then turn off the heat
11. Remove the swordfish from the grill and serve with caper sauce over it
12. Enjoy!

Nutrition Facts Per Serving

Calories: 472, Fat: 31 g, Saturated Fat: 6 g, Carbohydrates: 2 g, Fiber: 0.5 g, Sodium: 540 mg, Protein: 48 g

Chapter 6: Vegetarian and Vegan Recipes

Healthy Fruit Salad

(Prepping time: 5-10 minutes| Cooking time:4 minutes |For 4 servings)

Ingredients

- 1 can (9 ounces) pineapple chunks, drained, juice reserved
- 2 peaches, pitted and sliced
- ½ pound strawberries washed, hulled, and halved
- 1 tablespoon freshly squeezed lime juice
- 6 tablespoons honey, divided

Directions

1. Add strawberries, pineapple, peaches, and 3 tablespoons, honey, into a large bowl
2. Toss it well
3. Pre-heat Ninja Foodi by pressing the "GRILL" option and setting it to "MAX."
4. Set the timer to 15 minutes
5. Let it pre-heat until you hear a beep
6. Transfer fruits to Grill Grate and lock lid
7. Cook for 4 minutes
8. Add remaining 3 tablespoons of honey, lime juice, 1 tablespoon reserved pineapple juice into a small-sized bowl
9. Once cooked, place fruits in a large-sized bowl and toss with honey mixture
10. Serve and enjoy!

Nutrition Facts Per Serving

Calories: 178, Fat: 1 g, Saturated Fat: 0 g, Carbohydrates:47 g, Fiber: 3 g, Sodium: 3 mg, Protein: 2 g

Stuffed Up Cheesy Zucchini

(Prepping time: 5-10 minutes| Cooking time:8 minutes |For 3 servings)

Ingredients

- 1 zucchini
- 1 teaspoon olive oil
- ½ teaspoon tomato paste
- 5 ounces parmesan, shredded
- ½ teaspoon chili flakes
- ¼ teaspoon basil, dried

Directions

1. Take zucchini and cut into halves, scoop out the flesh from them
2. Spread tomato paste inside the halves
3. Add shredded cheese, sprinkle with chili flakes, dried basil, and olive oil
4. Pre-heat Ninja Foodi by pressing the "AIR CRISP" option and setting it to 375 Degrees F
5. Set the timer to 8 minutes
6. Let it pre-heat until you hear a beep
7. Arrange the prepared zucchini halves in Ninja Foodi Grill Basket
8. Cook for 8 minutes
9. Serve and enjoy!

Nutrition Facts Per Serving

Calories: 300, Fat: 21 g, Saturated Fat: 1 g, Carbohydrates: 6 g, Fiber: 1 g, Sodium: 459 mg, Protein: 12 g

Grilled Veggies with Mustard Vinaigrette

Prep time: 20 minutes, cook time: 15 minutes; Serves 10

Ingredients

- 1/2 teaspoon salt
- 1/8 teaspoon pepper
- 1/4 cup canola oil
- 1/4 cup red wine vinegar
- 1 tablespoon Dijon mustard
- 1 tablespoon honey
- 1/4 cup olive oil
- 2 large sweet onions
- 2 medium zucchini
- 2 yellow summer squash
- 2 large sweet red peppers, halved and seeded
- 1 bunch green onions, trimmed
- Cooking spray

Directions

1. In a bowl, whip the first 5 ingredients. Gradually whisk them in oil until blended.

2. Peel it and quarter each sweet onion, leaving the root ends intact. Cut the zucchini and yellow squash lengthwise into 1/2-in.-thick Slices. Lightly spritz onions, zucchini, yellow squash, and remaining vegetables with the cooking spray, turning to coat all sides.

3. Preheat the grill for five minutes before use.

4. Grill the sweet onions, covered, over medium heat 16-20 minutes until tender, turning occasionally. Grill the squash, zucchini, and peppers covered, over medium heat 11-15 minutes or until crisp-tender and lightly charred, turning once. Grill the green onions, covered, 3-4 minutes or until lightly charred, turning once.

5. Cut vegetables into bite-size pieces; place them in a big bowl. Add half cup vinaigrette and toss to coat. Serve with remaining vinaigrette.

Nutrition Facts Per Serving

Calories 168, Total Fat 12g, Total Carbs 13g, Protein 2g

Exciting Olive and Spinach

(Prepping time: 5-10 minutes| Cooking time:15 minutes |For 3 servings)

Ingredients

- 2 pounds spinach, chopped and boiled
- 4 tablespoons butter
- 2/3 cup Kalamata olives, halved and pitted
- 1 and ½ cups feta cheese, grated
- 4 teaspoons lemon zest, grated
- Pepper and salt to taste

Directions

1. Add spinach, butter, salt, pepper into a mixing bowl
2. Mix them well
3. Pre-heat Ninja Foodi by pressing the "AIR CRISP" option and setting it to "340 Degrees F."
4. Set the timer to 15 minutes
5. Let it pre-heat until you hear a beep
6. Arrange a reversible trivet in the Grill Pan
7. Arrange spinach mixture in a basket and place basket in the trivet
8. Roast it for 15 minutes
9. Serve and enjoy!

Nutrition Facts Per Serving

Calories: 250, Fat: 18 g, Saturated Fat: 3 g, Carbohydrates: 8 g, Fiber: 4 g, Sodium: 339 mg, Protein: 10 g

Bruschetta from the Grill

(Prepping time: 15 minutes| Cooking time: 5-10 minutes |For 8-10 servings)

Ingredients

- 3 tablespoons balsamic vinegar
- 3 tablespoons olive oil
- 1 pound plum tomatoes (about 6), seeded and chopped
- 1 cup chopped celery or fennel bulb
- 1/4 cup minced fresh basil
- 3 tablespoons Dijon mustard
- 2 garlic cloves, minced
- 1/2 teaspoon salt

Mayonnaise Spread:

- 1/2 cup mayonnaise
- 1 garlic clove, minced
- 3/4 teaspoon dried oregano
- 1/4 cup Dijon mustard
- 1 tablespoon finely chopped green onion
- 1 loaf (1 pound) French bread, cut into 1/2-inch slices

Directions

1. Take a large bowl and mix the first eight ingredients thoroughly. Cover and refrigerate for a minimum of 30 minutes. For mayonnaise spread, combine the mayonnaise, mustard, onion, garlic, and oregano in a small bowl; set aside.

2. Preheat the grill for 8 minutes before using it. Grill the bread slices while uncovered over medium-low heat for 1-2 minutes until lightly toasted. Turn the bread and spread with the mayonnaise mixture. Grill for 1-2 minutes longer or until bottoms of bread is toasted. Drain tomato mixture; spoon over tops.

Nutrition Facts Per Serving

Calories 279, Total Fat 15g, Total Carbs 28g, Total Protein 8g

Shishito Pepper Charred

(Prepping time: 10 minutes| Cooking time:10 minutes |For 4 servings)

Ingredients

- 3 cups Shishito peppers
- 2 tablespoons vegetable oil
- Salt to taste
- Pepper to taste

Directions

1. Select GRILL mode and set your Ninja Foodi Grill to "MAX."
2. Set timer to 10 minutes
3. Let it pre-heat until you hear a beep
4. Transfer pepper to grill grate and press peppers down and lock lid
5. Cook for 8-10 minutes
6. Once done, serve with some salt and pepper sprinkled on top
7. Serve and enjoy!

Nutrition Facts Per Serving

Calories: 83, Fat: 7 g, Saturated Fat: 2 g, Carbohydrates: 5 g, Fiber: 1 g, Sodium: 49 mg, Protein: 0

Blissful Simple Beans

(Prepping time: 5 minutes| Cooking time: 10 minutes |For 4 servings)

Ingredients

- 1-pound green beans, trimmed
- 1 lemon, juiced
- 2 tablespoons vegetable oil
- Flaky sea salt as needed
- Fresh ground black pepper as needed
- Pinch of red pepper flakes

Directions

1. Add green beans into a medium-sized bowl
2. Pre-heat your Ninja Foodi by pressing the "GRILL" option and setting it to "MAX."
3. Set the timer to 10 minutes
4. Allow it to pre-heat until you hear a beep
5. Once pre-heated, transfer green beans to Grill Grate
6. Close the lid
7. Grill for 8-10 minutes
8. Toss them from time to time until all sides are blustered well
9. Squeeze lemon juice over green beans
10. Top with red pepper flakes
11. Season with salt and pepper
12. Serve and enjoy!

Nutrition Facts Per Serving

Calories: 100, Fat: 7 g, Saturated Fat: 1 g, Carbohydrates: 10 g, Fiber: 4 g, Sodium: 30 mg, Protein: 2 g

Toasty Broccoli

(Prepping time: 5-10 minutes| Cooking time:15 minutes |For 3 servings)

Ingredients

- 1 large broccoli head, cut into florets
- 2 tablespoons parmesan, grated
- ½ teaspoon red pepper flakes
- 2 tablespoons extra virgin olive oil
- ¼ cup toasted almonds, sliced
- Lemon wedges
- Pepper and salt to taste

Directions

1. Add broccoli into a mixing bowl
2. Season with salt and pepper
3. Then add red pepper flakes and toss well
4. Pre-heat Ninja Foodi by pressing the "AIR CRISP" option and setting it to "390 Degrees F."
5. Set the timer to 15 minutes
6. Let it pre-heat until you hear a beep
7. Arrange a reversible trivet in the Grill Pan, arrange broccoli crisps in the trivet
8. Roast it for 15 minutes
9. Add cheese on top and some lemon wedges
10. Serve and enjoy!

Nutrition Facts Per Serving

Calories: 181, Fat: 11 g, Saturated Fat: 3 g, Carbohydrates: 9 g, Fiber: 4 g, Sodium: 421 mg, Protein: 8 g

Honey-Licious Asparagus

(Prepping time: 5-10 minutes| Cooking time:15 minutes |For 4 servings)

Ingredients

- 2 pounds asparagus, trimmed
- 4 tablespoons tarragon, minced
- ¼ cup honey
- 2 tablespoons olive oil
- 1 teaspoon salt
- ½ teaspoon pepper

Directions

1. Add asparagus, oil, salt, honey, pepper, tarragon into your bowl
2. Toss them well
3. Pre-heat your Ninja Foodi by pressing the "GRILL" option and setting it to "MED."
4. Set the timer to 8 minutes
5. Let it pre-heat until you hear a beep
6. Arrange asparagus over the grill grate
7. Lock the lid
8. Cook for 4 minutes
9. Then flip asparagus
10. Cook for 4 minutes more
11. Serve and enjoy!

Nutrition Facts Per Serving

Calories: 240, Fat: 15 g, Saturated Fat: 3 g, Carbohydrates: 31 g, Fiber: 1 g, Sodium: 103 mg, Protein: 7 g

Honey and Herb Charred Carrots

(Prepping time: 15 minutes| Cooking time:10 minutes |For 4-6 servings)

Ingredients

- 1 tablespoon honey
- 1 tablespoon fresh parsley, chopped
- 1 tablespoon fresh rosemary, chopped
- 1 teaspoon kosher salt
- 2 tablespoons melted butter
- 6 medium carrots, peeled, cut in lengthwise

Directions

1. Preheat for eight minutes.

2. Insert grill grate in the unit and close the hood. Select the option GRILL, set the temperature to MAX, and set time to ten minutes. Select the option START/STOP to begin preheating.

3. In a small bowl, stir together salt, honey, and melted butter.

4. Coat the carrots with honey butter, then rub it evenly with the fresh herbs.

5. When the unit starts beeping to signal that it has preheated, place carrots at the center on the grill grate. Close the hood and cook it for 5 minutes.

6. After five minutes, turn the carrots. Close the hood and cook it for the remaining five minutes.

7. When cooking is complete, serve immediately.

Nutrition Facts Per Serving

Calories 75, Total Fat 3.9g, Total Carbs 9.3g, Protein 0.6g

Broccoli and Torn Arugula

(Prepping time: 10 minutes| Cooking time: 12 minutes |For 4 servings)

Ingredients

- 4 cups arugula, torn
- 2 heads broccoli, trimmed into florets
- 1 tablespoon lemon juice
- 1 teaspoon honey
- 2 tablespoons parmesan cheese, grated
- ½ red onion, sliced
- 1 tablespoon canola oil
- 1 teaspoon Dijon mustard
- 1 garlic cloves, minced
- 2 tablespoons extra-virgin olive oil
- ¼ teaspoon of sea salt
- Red pepper flakes
- Black pepper, freshly grounded

Directions

1. Insert the grill grate and close the lid
2. Pre-heat Ninja Foodi by pressing the "GRILL" option and setting it to "MAX."
3. Set the timer to 12 minutes
4. Add broccoli, sliced onions, canola oil into a large bowl
5. Toss until coated well
6. Let it pre-heat until you hear a beep
7. Arrange the vegetables over the grill grate and lock lid
8. Cook for 8 to 12 minutes
9. Add lemon juice, mustard, olive oil, honey, garlic, red pepper flakes, salt, and pepper into a medium bowl
10. Whisk them together
11. Once cooked, combine the roasted vegetables and arugula in a large serving bowl
12. Drizzle with the vinaigrette to taste and sprinkle with parmesan cheese
13. Serve and enjoy!

Nutrition Facts Per Serving

Calories: 168, Fat: 12 g, Saturated Fat: 3 g, Carbohydrates: 13 g, Fiber: 1 g, Sodium: 392 mg, Protein: 6 g

Grilled Tomato Salsa

(Prepping time: 15 minutes| Cooking time:10 minutes |For 4 servings)

Ingredients

- 5 Roma tomatoes, cut in half lengthwise
- 1 tablespoon kosher salt
- 2 teaspoons ground black pepper
- 1 red onion, peeled, cut in quarters
- 1 jalapeño pepper, cut in half, seeds removed
- 3 cloves garlic, peeled
- 2 tablespoons ground cumin
- 2 tablespoons canola oil
- 1 bunch fresh cilantro, stems trimmed
- Juice and zest of 3 limes

Directions

1. Preheat for eight minutes.

2. In a big bowl, combine onion, tomatoes, jalapeño pepper, salt, and black pepper with canola oil. Mix them well to ensure vegetables are coated with oil and seasonings.

3. Insert grill grate in the unit and close the hood. Select the option GRILL, set the temperature to MAX, and set time to ten minutes. Select the option START/STOP to begin preheating.

4. When the unit starts beeping to signal that it has preheated, place steaks on the grill grate. Close the hood and cook it for five minutes.

5. After five minutes, flip the vegetables. Close the hood and then cook for the remaining five minutes.

6. When cooking is complete, remove the mixture from the unit and allow it to cool.

7. Transfer the mixture to a food processor. Add garlic, cilantro, cumin, and lime juice and zest. Pulse until desired consistency is reached. Serve immediately, or chill in the refrigerator first.

Nutrition Facts Per Serving

Calories 147, Total Fat 10.1g, Total Carbs 11.5g, Protein 2.5g

Italian Rosemary Potatoes

(Prepping time: 10 minutes| Cooking time:20 minutes |For 4 servings)

Ingredients

- 2 pounds baby red potatoes, quartered
- ¼ cup onion flakes, dried
- ½ teaspoon parsley, dried
- ¼ teaspoon celery powder
- 2 tablespoons extra virgin olive oil
- ½ teaspoon garlic powder
- ½ teaspoon salt
- ½ teaspoon onion powder
- ¼ teaspoon freshly ground black pepper

Directions

1. Add all listed ingredients into a large bowl
2. Toss well and coat them well
3. Pre-heat your Ninja Foodi by pressing the "AIR CRISP" option and setting it to 390 Degrees F
4. Set the timer to 20 minutes
5. Allow it to pre-heat until you hear a beep
6. Once pre-heated, add potatoes to the cooking basket
7. Close the lid and cook for 10 minutes
8. Shake the basket
9. Cook for 10 minutes more
10. Cook for 5 minutes more if needed
11. Serve and enjoy!

Nutrition Facts Per Serving

Calories: 232, Fat: 7 g, Saturated Fat: 1 g, Carbohydrates: 39 g, Fiber: 6 g, Sodium: 249 mg, Protein: 4 g

Spicy Grilled Eggplant

(Prepping time: 10 minutes| Cooking time: 10 minutes |For 6 servings)

Ingredients

- 1/4 cup olive oil
- 2 tablespoons lime juice
- 2 small eggplants, cut into 1/2-inch slices
- 3 teaspoons Cajun seasoning

Directions

1. Brush eggplant slices with oil. Sprinkle with lime juice and Cajun seasoning. Let it stand for 5 minutes.

2. Preheat the grill for 8 minutes before use. Grill the eggplant slices while covered over medium heat or broil 4 in from heat until tender, 4-5 minutes per side.

Nutrition Facts Per Serving

Calories 95, Total Fat 7g, Total Carbs 7g, Total Protein 1g

Rice & Vegetable Stuffed Peppers

(Prepping time: 15 minutes| Cooking time: 32 minutes |For 6 servings)

Ingredients

- 6 red or green bell peppers, top 1/2-inch sections cut off and reserved, seeds and ribs removed from the insides
- 4 cloves garlic, minced
- 1 package (1 ounce) fajita spice mix
- 1 can (10 ounces) red enchilada sauce
- 1 small white onion, peeled, diced
- 2 bags (8.5 ounces) instant rice, cooked in the microwave
- 1 can (4 ounces) diced green chilis, drained
- 1/2 cup vegetable stock
- 1 bag (8 ounces) shredded Colby Jack cheese, divided

Directions

1. Preheat for three minutes.
2. Chop the 1half-inch portions of the reserved bell peppers and place it in a mixing bowl. Combine all the remaining ingredients to the mixing bowl, except for the whole bell peppers and half the cheese.
3. Use a cooking pot without grill grate or crisper basket installed. Close the hood. Select the option ROAST, set the temperature to 350°F, and then set time to thirty-two minutes. Press the START button to begin preheating.
4. While the unit preheats, spoon the mixture into the peppers, fill them up as fully as possible. If necessary, lightly press the mixture into the peppers to fit more of them in it.
5. When the unit starts beeping to signal that it has preheated, put the peppers, standing straight, into the pot. Close the hood and then cook for thirty minutes.
6. After thirty minutes, evenly sprinkle the remaining cheese over the top of the peppers. Close the hood and cook it for the remaining two minutes.
7. Serve right after the cooking is complete.

Nutrition Facts Per Serving

Calories 513, Total Fat 13.9g, Total Carbs 81.1g, Protein 15.8g

Chapter 7: Desserts Recipes

Juicy Grilled Pound Cakes

(Prepping time: 5-10 minutes| Cooking time: 10 minutes |For 4 servings)

Ingredients

- 3 tablespoons unsalted butter, room temperature
- 6 slices pound cake, sliced 1-inch thick
- 1 cup fresh raspberries
- 1 cup fresh blueberries
- 3 tablespoons sugar
- ½ tablespoon fresh mint, minced

Directions

1. Spread butter on both sides of pound cake
2. Pre-heat your Ninja Foodi by selecting MAX mode on GRILL and set the timer to 8 minutes
3. Pre-heat until you hear a beep, place pound cake to Grill Grate, lock lid and cook for 2 minutes
4. Flip and cook for 2 minutes more
5. Repeat for all slices
6. Take a medium mixing bowl and add raspberries, sugar, blueberries,s mint
7. Once done, serve cake slice with berry mix
8. Enjoy!

Nutrition Facts Per Serving

Calories: 215, Fat: 12 g, Saturated Fat: 7 g, Carbohydrates: 27 g, Fiber: 2 g, Sodium: 161 mg, Protein: 2 g

Granola Flavored Healthy Muffin

(Prepping time: 10 minutes| Cooking time: 15-20 minutes |For 4 servings)

Ingredients

- 3 ounces plain granola
- 3 handful of cooked vegetables of your choice
- ¼ cup of coconut milk
- A handful of thyme diced
- 1 tablespoon coriander
- Salt and pepper to taste

Directions

1. Preheat Ninja Foodi by pressing the "AIR CRISP" option and setting it to "352 Degrees F" and timer to 20 minutes
2. Take a mixing bowl and add cooked vegetables
3. Take an immersion blender and whiz granola until you have a breadcrumb-like texture
4. Add coconut milk to the granola and add veggies
5. Mix well into muffin/ball shapes
6. Transfer them to preheated Ninja Foodi Grill and cook for 20 minutes
7. Serve and enjoy once done!

Nutrition Facts Per Serving

Calories: 140, Fat: 10 g, Saturated Fat: 3 g, Carbohydrates: 14 g, Fiber: 4 g, Sodium: 215 mg, Protein: 2 g

Marshmallow Banana Boat

(Prepping time: 19 minutes| Cooking time:6 minutes |For 4 servings)

Ingredients

- 4 ripe bananas
- 1 cup mini marshmallows
- ½ cup of chocolate chips
- ½ cup peanut butter chips

Directions

1. Slice a banana lengthwise, keeping its peel. Make sure to not cut all the way through
2. Use your hands to open banana peel like a book, revealing the inside of a banana
3. Divide marshmallow, chocolate chips, peanut butter among bananas, stuffing them inside
4. Preheat Ninja Foodi by pressing the "GRILL" option and setting it to "MEDIUM" and timer to 6 minutes
5. let it preheat until you hear a beep
6. Transfer banana to Grill Grate and lock lid, cook for 4-6 minutes until chocolate melts and bananas are toasted
7. Serve and enjoy!

Nutrition Facts Per Serving

Calories: 505, Fat: 18 g, Saturated Fat: 13 g, Carbohydrates: 82 g, Fiber: 6 g, Sodium: 103 mg, Protein: 10 g

Blueberry Cobbler Delight

(Prepping time: 5-10 minutes| Cooking time: 30 minutes |For 4 servings)

Ingredients

- 4 cups fresh blueberries
- 1 teaspoon lemon zest, grated
- 1 cup sugar + 2 tablespoons
- 1 cup all-purpose flour + 2 tablespoons extra
- 1 lemon, juiced
- 2 teaspoons baking powder
- ¼ teaspoon salt
- /6 tablespoons unsalted butter
- ¾ cup whole milk
- 1/8 teaspoon ground cinnamon

Directions

1. Take a medium-sized bowl, add blueberries, lemon zest, 2 tablespoons sugar, 2 tablespoons flour, and remaining lemon juice

2. Take a medium-sized bowl and add the remaining 1 cup flour, 1 cup sugar, baking powder, salt. Cut butter into flour mixture until it forms an even crumb texture, stir in milk until you have a nice dough

3. Pre-heat Ninja Foodi by pressing the "BAKE" option and setting it to "350 Degrees F" and timer to 30 minutes

4. let it pre-heat until you hear a beep

5. Take your multi-purpose pan and pour the blueberry mixture, spread evenly well

6. Pour batter over blueberry mixture, sprinkle cinnamon over top

7. Once done, transfer pan to your Grill and lock lid, bake for 30 minutes

8. Serve once done

9. Enjoy!

Nutrition Facts Per Serving

Calories: 405, Fat: 13 g, Saturated Fat: 8 g, Carbohydrates: 72 g, Fiber: 3 g, Sodium: 194 mg, Protein: 5 g

Excellent Rum Sundae

(Prepping time: 5-10 minutes| Cooking time: 8 minutes |For 4 servings)

Ingredients

- ½ cup dark rum
- ½ cup brown sugar, packed
- 1 teaspoon cinnamon, ground
- 1 pineapple, cored and sliced
- Vanilla ice cream for serving

Directions

1. Take a large-sized bowl and add sugar, rum, and cinnamon
2. Add pineapple in the layer, dredge them, and coat well
3. Pre-heat your Ninja Foodi to MAX and set the timer to 8 minutes
4. Once you hear the beep, strain any rum from pineapple slices and transfer them to the grill grate
5. Cook for 6-8 minutes; cook in batches if needed
6. Top each ring with a scoop of ice cream and sprinkle cinnamon
7. Enjoy!

Nutrition Facts Per Serving

Calories: 240, Fat: 4 g, Saturated Fat: 1 g, Carbohydrates: 43 g, Fiber: 8 g, Sodium: 85 mg, Protein: 2 g

The Original Corn Biscuit

(Prepping time: 10 minutes| Cooking time: 15-20 minutes |For 4 servings)

Ingredients

- 2/3 cup buttermilk
- 1/3 cup vegetable shortening
- ½ teaspoon salt
- 2 and ½ teaspoon baking powder
- ½ cup yellow cornmeal
- 1 and ½ cups all-purpose flour, plus more

Directions

1. In a large-sized bowl, take flour, cornmeal, baking powder, salt
2. Then respectively add shortening, until it is well-combined, cut into the flour mixture, and the dough resembles fine coarse meal
3. Onward add buttermilk and stir continually until moist
4. Press the "AIR CRISP" option and set this in "350 Degrees F" to pre-heat Ninja Foodi with a 15 minutes timer
5. Until you hear a beep, keep it in the pre-heat process
6. When it is done, take some flour, dust on a clean work surface until cohesive dough forms, knead the mixture on a floured surface
7. Through that dough, roll out in a thick form and cut with a 2-inch biscuit cutter
8. Grease well of your crisper basket, place 6-8 biscuits in the basket
9. Put into the Grill and bake for 12-15 minutes until golden brown
10. Take out biscuits from the basket and repeat with remaining dough
11. Serve and enjoy!

Nutrition Facts Per Serving

Calories: 265, Fat: 12 g, Carbohydrates: 34 g, Protein: 5 g, Sodium: 310 mg, Fiber: 6 g, Saturated Fat: 4 g

Air Crisped Delicious Mac and Cheese

(Prepping time: 5-10 minutes| Cooking time: 10 minutes |For 4 servings)

Ingredients

- 1 tablespoon parmesan cheese, grated
- Salt and pepper
- 1 and ½ cheddar cheese, grated
- ½ cup milk, warmed
- ½ cup broccoli
- 1 cup elbow macaroni

Directions

1. Pre-heat Ninja Foodi by pressing the "AIR CRISP" option and setting it to "400 Degrees F" and timer to 10 minutes
2. let it pre-heat until you hear a beep
3. Take a pot and add water, allow it to boil
4. Add macaroni and veggies and broil for about 10 minutes until the mixture is Al Dente
5. Drain the pasta and vegetables
6. Toss the pasta and veggies with cheese
7. Season with some pepper and salt and transfer the mixture to your Foodi
8. Sprinkle some more parmesan on top and cook for about 15 minutes.
9. Allow it to cool for about 10 minutes once done
10. Enjoy!

Nutrition Facts Per Serving

Calories: 180, Fat: 11 g, Saturated Fat: 3 g, Carbohydrates: 14 g, Fiber: 2 g, Sodium: 147 mg, Protein: 6 g

Rummy Pineapple Sunday

(Prepping time: 10 minutes| Cooking time:8 minutes |For 4 servings)

Ingredients

- ½ cup dark rum
- ½ cup packed brown sugar
- 1 teaspoon ground cinnamon, plus more for garnish
- 1 pineapple cored and sliced
- Vanilla ice cream, for serving

Directions

1. Take a large-sized bowl and add rum, sugar, cinnamon
2. Add pineapple slices, arrange them in the layer. Coat mixture then let them soak for 5 minutes, per side
3. Preheat Ninja Foodi by pressing the "GRILL" option and setting it to "MAX" and timer to 8 minutes
4. let it preheat until you hear a beep
5. Strain extra rum sauce from pineapple
6. Transfer prepared fruit in grill grate in a single layer, press down fruit and lock lid
7. Grill for 6-8 minutes without flipping, work in batches if needed
8. Once done, remove and top each pineapple ring with a scoop of ice cream, sprinkle cinnamon and serve
9. Enjoy!

Nutrition Facts Per Serving

Calories: 240, Fat: 4 g, Saturated Fat: 2 g, Carbohydrates: 43 g, Fiber: 3 g, Sodium: 32 mg, Protein: 2 g

Fiery Cajun Eggplant Dish

(Prepping time: 5-10 minutes| Cooking time:12 minutes |For 4 servings)

Ingredients

- 2 tablespoons lime juice
- 3 teaspoons Cajun seasoning
- 2 small eggplants, cut into slices
- ¼ cup olive oil

Directions

1. Coat eggplant slices with oil, lemon juice, and Cajun seasoning
2. Take your Ninja Foodi Grill and press "GRILL" and set to "MED" mode, set the timer to 10 minutes
3. Let it preheat
4. Arrange eggplants over grill grate, lock lid and cook for 5 minutes
5. Flip and cook for 5 minutes more
6. Serve and enjoy!

Nutrition Facts Per Serving

Calories: 362, Fat: 11 g, Saturated Fat: 3 g, Carbohydrates: 16 g, Fiber: 1 g, Sodium: 694 mg, Protein: 8 g

Flattering Banana Chips

(Prepping time: 5-10 minutes| Cooking time: 15 minutes |For 4 servings)

Ingredients

- 1 teaspoon olive oil
- ½ teaspoon Chaat Masala
- ½ teaspoon turmeric powder
- 1 teaspoon salt
- 3-4 raw banana

Directions

1. Pre-heat your Ninja Foodi to 352 degrees F, in AIR CRISP mode, set the timer to 15 minutes
2. Peel the skin off the bananas, keep them on the side
3. Take a bowl and add salt, powder, turmeric, water
4. Cut banana slices into the mix, soak for 10 minutes
5. Drain the chips and dry them
6. Add a bit of oil on top
7. Transfer them to Ninja Grill basket and Grill for 15 minutes
8. Serve and enjoy!

Nutrition Facts Per Serving

Calories: 305, Fat: 14 g, Saturated Fat: 3 g, Carbohydrates: 30 g, Fiber: 3 g, Sodium: 164 mg, Protein: 4 g

Premium Tomato and Bacon Omelet

(Prepping time: 5-10 minutes| Cooking time: 10 minutes |For 4 servings)

Ingredients

- Salt and pepper to taste
- 1 tablespoon olive oil
- 1 tablespoon parsley, chopped
- 4 tomatoes, cubed
- ¼ pound cubed, cooked, and chopped
- 1 tablespoon cheddar, grated
- 4 whole eggs, whisked

Directions

1. Take a small-sized pan and place it over medium heat, add bacon and Saute for 2 minutes until crispy

2. Take a bowl and add bacon, alongside the remaining ingredients

3. Stir well, sprinkle cheese on top

4. Pre-heat your Ninja Foodi to 400 degrees F in BAKE mode, set timer to 10 minutes

5. Pour mixture into a baking dish, transfer baking dish to Ninja Foodi Grill

6. Bake for 8 minutes

7. Serve and enjoy!

Nutrition Facts Per Serving

Calories: 311, Fat: 16 g, Saturated Fat: 4 g, Carbohydrates: 23 g, Fiber: 4 g, Sodium: 149 mg, Protein: 22 g